How Schools Can Help Combat

# Student Drug and Alcohol Abuse

## The Author

Richard L. Towers is Director of Interagency, Alternative, and Supplementary Programs for the Montgomery County, Maryland, public schools. A former classroom teacher, building administrator, and assistant superintendent of schools, Dr. Towers has also taught at the university level and acted as a consultant in programming for students with special needs. He has been involved in drug and alcohol abuse prevention since 1970, when he served as a community volunteer for the Freeport, Long Island, Narcotics Guidance Council.

How Schools Can Help Combat

# Student Drug and Alcohol Abuse

*by Richard L. Towers*



nea PROFESSIONAL LIBRARY
National Education Association
Washington, D.C.

**Note**

The opinions expressed in this publication should not be construed as representing the policy or position of the National Education Association. Materials published as part of the NEA Combat Series are intended to be discussion documents for teachers who are concerned with specialized interests of the profession.

**Library of Congress Cataloging-in-Publication Data**

Towers, Richard L.
How schools can help combat student drug and alcohol abuse.

(How schools can help combat series)
Bibliography: p.
1. Alcoholism—Study and teaching—United States.
2. Drug abuse—Study and teaching—United States.
3. Students—United States—Alcohol use. 4. Students—United States—Drug use. 5. Alcoholism—Treatment—United States. 6. Drug abuse—Treatment—United States.
I. Title. II. Series.
HV5128.U5T68 1987 362.2'9'071073 86-16471
ISBN 0-8106-3291-8

*To those young people who have been able to stop using drugs, to those who have helped them to stop, and to those teachers and other school employees who want to help make sure others never start, this book is dedicated.*

# NEA Policies on Substance Abuse

## NEA Resolutions

### B–42. Substance Abuse

The National Education Association is concerned about the individual and societal problems that underlie psychological and physiological drug—including alcohol and tobacco—dependency by both children and adults. It calls for new and improved ways of helping children and adults learn more positive ways of meeting and coping with these problems. It recognizes the need for improved educational programs about drugs and for the uniform categorization of drugs. It urges its affiliates to support legislation leading to the standardization of drug laws, which should not be limited to the sale and distribution of drugs, but should also include prohibition of the production, sale, and distribution of drug paraphernalia, and the improvement of drug rehabilitation programs.

The Association urges its affiliates to support legislation mandating drug rehabilitation programs for any violation or conviction, whether civil or criminal, resulting from the possession or use of a controlled substance.

The Association discourages the use of marijuana, except for prescribed medical purposes, and believes that severe penalties for its production, distribution, and sale should be strictly enforced.

The Association supports strict enforcement of the legal drinking age and the laws governing the sale of alcoholic beverages in each state and supports federal legislation to establish a uniform legal drinking age of 21. (72, 85)

### H–29. Highway Safety

The National Education Association believes that people should be protected from death and injury that result from the operation of motor vehicles by drivers under the influence of alcohol, drugs, or other mind-altering substances. To this end, the Association urges its members and affiliates to—

a. Support enactment and enforcement of effective and equitable legislation regulating driving while under the influence

b. Advocate appropriate educational experiences for students regarding the effects of driving while under the influence

c. Support recognized community and school groups in their efforts to reduce death and injury from accidents caused by drivers under the influence

d. Support legislation requiring mandatory restraint of all passengers in motor vehicles. (82, 86)

**B–38. Student Stress**

The National Education Association believes that there are increasing mental, emotional, and environmental pressures upon the children of this nation. These pressures—resulting in increased drug and alcohol abuse, violence, vandalism, dropping out of school, and suicide among children—speak clearly to the waste of human potential.

The Association urges its local and state affiliates to support appropriately accredited and licensed mental health and aftercare programs.

The Association further urges local and state affiliates to seek legislative support and publicity for these programs. (80, 85)

# NEA New Business Item

**Rehabilitation Centers for Juvenile Substance Abusers**

The National Education Association supports the establishment of substance abuse rehabilitation centers specifically designed to help juvenile substance abusers and their families. The Association urges its state affiliates to support actively legislation which will lead to the creation of such juvenile substance abuse centers, and/or which mandates the referral to such centers' programs of all juveniles found guilty by the courts of use or possession of a controlled substance. (1984–77)

## The Advisory Panel

Tom Ahern, English and Latin teacher, Barnstable High School, Hyannis, Massachusetts

Pilar Alfaro, Drug Abuse Coordinator, Andromeda Hispano Mental Health Center, Washington, D.C.

David Bell, Director, Teacher Education, Arkansas College, Batesville

Sarabeth King Blanck, Junior High School Librarian (retired), Richardson, Texas

James Boehlke, Guidance Counselor, Washington High School, Two Rivers, Wisconsin

Alice Chin, Program Director, Chinatown Planning Council, Asian Family Services, New York

Neil Chivington, School Social Worker, MSAD #6, Bar Mills, Maine

Earl D. Clark, Associate Professor, Curriculum, University of Alaska, Juneau

Deborah S. Firkser, Attendance/Computer Services, Elizabeth High School, New Jersey

Patricia A. Gazda-Grace, Guidance Counselor, Binghamton High School, New York

Mary L. Gleb, Librarian/Media Specialist, McMurray Intermediate School, Vashon, Washington

Ron Head, Program Specialist, American Indian Offices, Chemical Dependency Division, Department of Human Services, Minneapolis, Minnesota

Evelyn Herrero, Educational Consultant, San Juan, Puerto Rico

Stephen G. Hoppin, School Psychologist, Jefferson County Public Schools, Colorado

Richard L. Hughes, School Psychologist, Jewell Elementary School and Gateway High School, Aurora, Colorado

Francene Kaplan, Instructor, Huntington Beach Union High School Department of Alternative Education, California

Magda Leon, Multicultural Career Internship Program, Lincoln Junior High School, Washington, D.C.

Stanley M. Lucas, mathematics teacher, Gainesville High School, Florida

Kathy A. Martin, art teacher, Franklin County High School, Winchester, Tennessee

Meredith Monteville, Counselor, Solomon Elementary School, Wahiawa, Hawaii

Gwendolyn Parrott Phipps, Social Sciences-Career Education teacher, Johnson Elementary School, Rome, Georgia

Barbara Shaw Sneed, Counselor, East Gate Middle School, Ozark, Alabama

Vivian Young, Project Coordinator, Chinatown Alcoholism Project, New York

Dorothy Zaumseil, Elementary School Counselor and Psychometrician, Bedford, New Hampshire

# CONTENTS

CHAPTER 5

## ATTACKING the PROBLEM 68



CHAPTER 6

## PREVENTING STUDENT DRUG ABUSE 96



CHAPTER 7

## PREVENTION MATERIALS and ACTIVITIES for the CLASSROOM 128



CHAPTER 8

## PARENT, STUDENT, and COMMUNITY PREVENTION 160

# Foreword

Long ago I learned that if I wanted my students to absorb instructional material, I had to attend—closely and caringly—to their noninstructional needs. All of us in education have been forced—by cataclysmic shifts in our nation's social climate—to redefine our mission. We cannot hide from the fact that drug abuse, pregnancy, depression, anxiety, and suicide are part of our students' world. Mastery of the three R's presupposes the ability to cope.

In this book on combating drug and alcohol abuse among students, Dr. Richard L. Towers makes these points: that drugs can and will destroy many of our students; that teachers and other school employees must join with parents and others in the community to combat this threat; that the same problems and conditions that are in part responsible for drug abuse also contribute to teen pregnancy, vandalism, and suicide; and that there are any number of steps we can take, as classroom teachers, counselors, administrators, secretaries, and custodians, in the everyday course of events to help combat the problem.

I believe today's school employees understand well the close kinship between emotional maturity and academic mastery. That's why so much of their effort goes toward helping students acquire the self-esteem that is the prerequisite for mature development. Good teachers believe in students. In fact, they believe in students more than students believe in themselves. They know that for so many of our young people, the barriers to achievement are not intellectual but attitudinal. The barriers are low self-esteem, a shortage of confidence, the conviction that they don't have what it takes.

These attitudes are the enemies of learning as are the societal factors pressuring students to abuse their bodies with drugs and alcohol.

They're impediments to the achievement of full potential. The struggle to defeat those enemies and remove those impediments is an essential part of teaching. More precisely, that struggle is an essential part of creating a school climate in which students know they are valued and that they are not alone. Teachers cannot accomplish this on their own. The climate that soothes bruised egos, bolsters sagging self-esteem, and helps prevent youngsters from turning to drugs is the product of a schoolwide effort and of a partnership with the home and the community.

Just how we go about forming this partnership and making this effort can be found in the following pages. In them, Dr. Towers provides usable, specific strategies, materials, and references for elementary as well as secondary school personnel. I commend this volume to you whatever your role in the school, whatever age or condition the children with whom you work. You may turn directly to the classroom or schoolwide activities, picking and choosing, or you may begin at the front of this book and read on to the end. However you decide to use the book, all the chapters in it are useful and represent a basic level of understanding that all school employees should attain regarding the drug/alcohol problem our students face.

—Mary Hatwood Futrell
President, NEA
August 1986

# Preface

This book was written for all persons who work in schools, but it can be useful to anyone who works with children and youth and cares about their welfare and achievement. It was written to fill a void.

After an overall decline over several years, the use of drugs and alcohol by adolescents may once again be rising.[i]* The average age of initial drug use continues to reach downward to the elementary school.[ii] Fourth graders report substantial peer pressure to try drugs and alcohol.[iii] The major sources of information on the dangers of drugs and alcohol for fourth and fifth graders are their families, television, and films.[iv] From grade 2 to grade 9, the percentage of kids who like school "a lot" drops drastically, from over 60 percent to less than 20 percent.[v] Twenty to 40 percent of the students in our schools have a parent who abuses drugs or alcohol, putting them at risk of developing a variety of problems, including that of becoming drug abusers themselves.[vi] For students who abuse drugs, their motivation and ability to learn, their acquisition of needed social and emotional skills, and their very lives are in jeopardy. Yet few school employees know what to do about the problem, or if they should do anything about it. Many are not even aware of the problem.

This book gives readers a basic understanding of drugs and their effects on mind and body, but it does not dwell on pharmacology or on statistics. It reviews the stages of chemical dependency and the vocabulary of the drug scene, as well

---

*Superior numbers appearing in the text refer to the References beginning on page 210.

as the reasons kids take drugs and the telltale signs of student drug use. It also notes the interrelationship of drug use, behavior problems, eating disorders, chronic truancy, teenage pregnancy, running away, and delinquency. (The term "drug" as used in the book means "drugs and alcohol," unless otherwise specified.) Throughout, the emphasis is on the importance of schools' assuming their share of the ownership for the student drug abuse problem along with parents, students, government, and business, as well as on the need to build coalitions with these groups.

The major portion of the book is devoted to methods of preventing student abuse of drugs and alcohol and what to do about it when abuse occurs. Descriptions of a number of activities, materials, and programs that schools around the country have found useful are included. The absence of a program or approach, however, does not imply a lack of effectiveness. Fortunately, the number of materials and programs designed to prevent and combat student drug use is increasing in both quality and quantity. Social scientists who have studied the problem now generally accept the school's unique access to the great majority of youth and its potential to affect students' drug usage.

The book also presents an overview of treatment programs and reviews the school's role in aftercare and reentry to school for recovering drug abusers. It does not, however, discuss issues of codependency, the use of positive peer pressure, confrontational strategies, and other counseling techniques beyond its scope.

Care has been taken to make this volume relevant and useful for those who work with elementary as well as those who work with secondary school students; urban as well as suburban and rural; American Indian/Alaska Native, Asian/Pacific Islander, Black, Chicano/Hispanic, and white; and students from the South and West as well as those from the North and East. The advice and suggestions contained in the following pages do not constitute legal advice; and the reader is encouraged to consult local and state policies, regulations, and legislation. Likewise, because of differences in local conditions, the materials, programs, and practices proved successful in one school may not be appropriate or desirable for all others. The addresses and telephone numbers at the end of each chapter will be helpful. Once readers begin to explore a topic, they will be amazed at how much is available, even in their own backyard.

In addition to the dedicated members of the NEA Advisory Panel for the original manuscript, many friends and colleagues provided valuable advice and support. They include but are not limited to Dr. Cao An Quan, Charles E. D'Aiutolo, Margit Meissner, Rita Rumbaugh, Helen Chaset, Mary Blair Shaw, Claudia Meltzer, H. Brian Berthiaume, and the staff and students of the Phoenix I and Phoenix II programs. I would also like to recognize the influence of my mother, Mrs. Jean Towers, whose genuine concern for others has had a major impact on my development as an educator and as an individual. Finally, I am grateful to my wife, Judy, and children, Rachel, Karin, and Adrienne, for their tolerance and understanding of my absence and inattention during the many evenings and weekends it took to complete this project.

—Richard L. Towers

CHAPTER 1

# The Drug Abuse Problem

I think of PCP as the armpit of drugs.

—Detective Ray Brett
D.C. Police
Narcotics Squad

If you teach high school, the chances are that about one-fourth of the students in your classes regularly smoke marijuana, more than two-thirds regularly use alcohol, and approximately one-fifth drink on a daily basis.[1] Teenagers in the United States have the highest rate of drug abuse of any industrialized country in the world, and the percentage of our youth who commit suicide has tripled in the last 20 years. The abuse of drugs and alcohol figures prominently in these statistics.

Nor are younger children immune: the beginning average ages of marijuana use and alcohol drinking have now dropped to 11 and 12 years of age respectively.[2]

If these figures are shocking and disturbing, we are on our way to realizing two of the three major goals of this book:

- To raise education employees' awareness of the drug/alcohol problem among children and youth
- To motivate education employees to want to become a part of the solution.

The third and perhaps most important goal is to give education employees practical, concrete information that they can use to combat drug and alcohol abuse among students in their schools and communities. First, however, let us look at the nature of the problem.

Drugs that children take can kill, cripple, and ruin young lives. In addition to serious physical damage, drugs can also cause tremendous emotional damage. Users learn to use drugs as substitutes for coping with life's problems. When the drugs are not available, the youngster's ability to deal with life disappears also. Drug use, then, becomes the central focus of the abuser's existence. About 5,000 adolescents commit suicide each year—or about 13 each day—and a half-million more attempt it.[3] Whether drug use is directly responsible is unproven, but we know that many of the same kinds of problems and pressures that cause adolescents to try drugs also cause them to attempt suicide. Indeed, surveys show that drug abusers account for much of the recent rise in teenage suicides.[4] Experience tells us that most young people who abuse drugs have lower grades and are involved in more delinquency.[5]

## Commonly Abused Drugs and Their Effects

### Illegal Drugs

Almost any chemical substance can be used to abuse the body and probably has been used in that way at some time or other. Table 1 lists some commonly abused substances that the U.S. government has designated as "controlled substances" under the Comprehensive Drug Abuse and Control Act of 1970. This law makes it illegal for anyone to manufacture, distribute, or even possess these substances with the intention of distributing them to others without proper authorization. Punishments for violating the law can be quite severe, ranging up to 30 years in prison and $50,000 in fines.

The first category of controlled substance, *narcotics*, refers to opium and its derivatives or synthetic substitutes. Often these are listed as

# TABLE 1. CONTROLLED SUBSTANCES:

| | Drugs | Trade or Other Names | Medical Uses | Duration of Effects (in hours) |
|---|---|---|---|---|
| NARCOTICS | Opium | Dover's Powder, Paregoric Parepectolin | Analgesic, antidiarrheal | 3–6 |
| | Morphine | Morphine, Pectoral Syrup | Analgesic, antitussive | |
| | Codeine | Codeine, Empirin Compound with Codeine, Robitussin AC | Analgesic, antitussive | |
| | Heroin | Diacetylmorphine, Horse, Smack | Under investigation | |
| | Hydromorphone | Dilaudid | Analgesic | |
| | Meperidine (Pethidine) | Demerol, Pethadol | Analgesic | |
| | Methadone | Dolophine, Methadone, Methadose | Analgesic, heroin substitute | 12–24 |
| DEPRESSANTS | Chloral Hydrate | Noctec, Somnos | Hypnotic | 5–8 |
| | Barbiturates | Amobarbital, Phenobarbital, Butisol, Phenoxbarbital, Secobarbital, Tuinal | Anesthetic, anticonvulsant sedative, hypnotic | 1–16 |
| | Glutethimide | Doriden | Sedative, hypnotic | 4–8 |
| | Methaqualone | Optimil, Parest, Quaalude, Somnafac, Sopor | | |
| STIMULANTS | Cocaine | Coke, Flake, Snow, Toot | Local anesthetic | 1–2 |
| | Amphetamines | Biphetamine, Delcobese, Desoxyn, Dexedrine, Mediatric | Hyperkinesis, narcolepsy, weight control | 2–4 |
| | Phenmetrazine | Preludin | | |
| | Methylphenidate | Ritalin | | |
| HALLUCINOGENS | LSD | Acid, Microdot | None | 8–12 |
| | Mescaline & Peyote | Mesc, Buttons, Cactus | | |
| | Phencyclidine | PCP, Angel Dust, Hog | Veterinary anesthetic | Variable |
| | Phencyclidine Analogs | PCE, PCPy, TCP | None | |
| | Other Hallucinogens | | | |
| CANNABIS | Marijuana | Pot, Acapulco Gold, Grass, Reefer, Sinsemilla, Thai Sticks | Under investigation | 2–4 |
| | Hashish | Hash | None | |

*Adapted from *Drugs of Abuse*, U.S. Department of Justice, Drug Enforcement Administration, 1979.

# USES AND EFFECTS *

| Physical Dependence | Psychological Dependence | Tolerance | Usual Methods of Administration | Possible Effects | Effects of Overdose |
|---|---|---|---|---|---|
| High | High | Yes | Oral, smoked | Exaggerated mood swings, euphoria, drowsiness, respiratory depression, constricted pupils, nausea | Slow and shallow breathing, clammy skin, convulsions, coma, possible death |
| | | | Oral, injected, smoked | | |
| Moderate | Moderate | | Oral, injected | | |
| High | High | | Injected, sniffed, smoked | | |
| | | | Oral, injected | | |
| Moderate | Moderate | Possible | Oral | Impaired thinking, memory, & judgment; slurred speech; disorientation; drunken behavior without odor of alcohol | Shallow respiration, cold & clammy skin, dilated pupils, weak & rapid pulse, coma, possible death |
| High to moderate | High to moderate | Yes | Oral, injected | | |
| High | High | | | | |
| Possible | High | Possible | Sniffed, smoked, injected | Increased alertness, excitation, euphoria, increased pulse rate & blood pressure, insomnia, loss of appetite | Agitation, increase in body temperature, hallucinations, convulsions, possible death |
| | | Yes | Oral, injected | | |
| None | Degree unknown | Yes | Oral | Illusions & hallucinations, poor perception of time & distance | Longer, more intense "trip" episodes, psychosis, possible death |
| | | | Oral, injected | | |
| Degree unknown | High | | Smoked, oral, injected | | |
| | Degree unknown | | | | |
| None | | Possible | | | |
| Degree unknown | Moderate | Yes | Smoked, oral | Euphoria, relaxed inhibitions, increased appetite, disoriented behavior | Fatigue, paranoia, possible psychosis |

opiates and grouped with depressants since they can have a depressing or sedative effect on the central nervous system and brain. The best known and most feared of this group is heroin, a substance often diluted with sugar, soap powder, or talcum before being distributed on the street.

The second category, *depressants* (downers), induces a state of intoxication remarkably like that of alcohol when taken in excessive amounts. As with narcotics, drugs in this group generally are both physically and psychologically addictive; that is, they will produce extreme physical symptoms such as nausea, insomnia, and delirium, as well as debilitating emotional dysfunction if the user is deprived of the substance. The most commonly abused drugs in this category include barbiturates, Quaaludes, Valium, and Librium.

The third category, *stimulants* (uppers), includes powerfully reinforcing drugs that can lead to increasingly compulsive behavior. So called for their effect on the nervous system, stimulants release adrenaline, increase blood pressure, and heighten awareness. Among this group is cocaine, the most potent stimulant of natural origin and the most increasingly popular drug in the United States today. Stimulants are extremely habit forming. Because the "high" is so intense and lasts such a relatively short time before the user wants to experience it again, the user often takes depressants along with the stimulant to soften the "crash" or to end the "high."

*Hallucinogens* (psychedelics) are natural and synthetic substances that distort the user's perception of reality. They can cause panic, paranoia, and possible long-term insanity. This group includes PCP, a drug that poses great risks to the user. The range of its effects is both bizarre and volatile, often producing psychosis indistinguishable from schizophrenia.

*Cannabis* is the category containing marijuana, which, along with alcohol, is the most abused drug in the United States. Marijuana is credited by many experts with leading youngsters into drug dependence since it often is the first illegal drug they try. At one time thought to be a benign substance whose moderate use should be decriminalized, marijuana use now is generally considered to be not only deceptively harmful to the psyche but a great risk to physical health as well. Lung damage from smoking "pot" is estimated to be 17 times greater than that caused by tobacco cigarettes. Marijuana sold on the street today is known to be 25 times more potent than that generally available to adolescents ten years ago. Prolonged heavy use of marijuana also can inhibit the development of coping skills needed to be a functional adult and can slow down memory, coordination, and reproductive abilities. Indeed, some experts credit marijuana with impeding the learning process by interfering with five elements necessary for learning to occur: (1) a prepared mind (one capable of receiving and integrating what is to be learned); (2) an intact memory; (3) the act of repeating, or practicing, the information or skill to be learned; (4) motivation; and (5) reinforcement or reward.[6]

## "Legal" Drugs

Psychologically active drugs, those that alter moods or perceptions of reality, are all around us—in medicines and in household products. Certain ones, like alcohol and tobacco, are accepted and institutionalized by society. Recently, adolescents and preadolescents in some areas have been increasingly inhaling glues and fumes from aerosol cans for a "cheap high," a practice that can lead to suffocation and death. Youngsters may raid the family medicine cabinet for barbiturates (which act as depressants), tranquilizers, or amphetamines (which may be prescribed for fatigue, depression, or obesity).

Alcohol is another powerful depressant. It can cause both physical and psychological dependence and may lead to brain and liver damage. Excessive intake by either parent around the time of conception or by the mother during pregnancy may severely harm the fetus. Alcohol use by teenagers tends to increase dramatically as they get older. Beer is by far their favorite beverage of abuse, followed by wine and hard liquor. Most adolescents are introduced to alcohol by experimenting with beer. As of this writing, drinking alcoholic beverages is illegal in all states for youngsters under the age of 18, and in 38 states for those under the age of 21.

Drinking to intoxication, or being "bombed" or "smashed," is a common occurrence among frequent adolescent users of alcohol. Of the 10 million alcoholics in this country an estimated 3.3 million are children. Another 12 to 23 million children currently live in homes with an alcoholic parent. Alcohol is a major problem for young drinkers—often leading to the use of other drugs. It is also a major physical and emotional problem for the children of alcoholics who face high risks of becoming alcoholics themselves.[7]

The direct relationship between smoking and cancer, heart disease, and other ailments such as emphysema has been well documented. Overall, during the last decade cigarette smoking has declined in the United States as more Americans have become conscious of and more concerned with their personal health. But while adults have been smoking less and exercising more, teenagers have been smoking more and exercising less; and teenage girls have been smoking more than teenage boys. The terrible future toll of this practice is even now showing up in higher lung cancer rates for women.

Another tobacco product that is particularly popular with athletes is chewing (a.k.a. "smokeless") tobacco or "snuff." Because this substance is advertised by professional sports figures, adolescents assume that its use cannot be too harmful. They are not aware that it can lead to cancer of the lip, cheek, tongue, and throat, causing disfigurement and death. Estimates of the number of teens "dipping" snuff range from 8 to 30 percent. It should also be noted that while cigarette ads are banned from television, smokeless tobacco ads are unregulated.

## "Designer" Drugs

Without question, the problem of drug abuse in this country is a big one—the United States consumes more illegal drugs than any other developed country—and the profits from drug traffic are enormous. Domestically grown marijuana, for example, is a $14-billion-a-year industry and is said to be the nation's number one cash crop.[8] The profits from cocaine and other drugs smuggled in from South America, the Orient, and Europe have become so huge they are said to have corrupted bankers, police, judges, and officials at all levels.[9]

American ingenuity and know-how have recently devised a new way to evade the law and make money—with "designer" drugs. These synthetic drugs, or analogs of similar controlled or illegal drugs, are different enough from the real thing to avoid being considered "controlled substances," thus freeing their dealers and manufacturers from drug trafficking penalties. Designer drugs simulate the effects of certain illegal drugs by changing the substance's chemical composition. The problem is that even a slight change in the chemical structure of a substance can increase its potency—and the chances of fatally overdosing. Certain analogs of a heroin-like narcotic called fentanyl are up to 1,500 times more potent than morphine; they have been sold on the street as "china white," "synthetic heroin," and "heroin."[10]

Some designer drugs have caused serious side effects such as brain damage and death. One analog of Demerol has left many of its users with the shaking symptoms of Parkinson's disease; other designer drugs have produced symptoms of similarly terrible diseases. The point is that when teens buy illegal drugs, they do not know what they are getting—and most times neither does the seller or friend who supplied them. From analogs made by underground kitchen chemists to marijuana sprayed with herbicides, the users of street drugs today are playing Russian roulette with their brains.

### Multiple Drug Use

Increasingly, teenagers are using a variety of drugs. Most alarming is the indiscriminate combining of interactive chemicals. Mixing alcohol with barbiturates and other substances that depress the central nervous system can, for example, bring on respiratory and heart failure. Counterbalancing uppers and downers, stimulants and depressants, is another frequent practice and can produce violent behavior.[11]

Adolescent drug abusers frequently use whatever happens to be available when they are ready to "party." Since young people often rely on friends for drugs, they cannot always control the drug they use. When they have reached the stage of drug dependence, students may have gone beyond the point where they care about what drug they use, as long as it provides a high, or "mellows" them beyond concern. The effects of mixed drug use on judgment and inhibitions can have disastrous results.

## Victimless Crime?

What if some young people destroy their minds and bodies with drugs? Why all the fuss? As some adolescents say, "It's my life. If I want to mess it up, it's my right." The fact is, of course, they are not the only ones who suffer the consequences. Adolescents addicted to drugs steal, assault, sell drugs to others, and sexually prostitute themselves to support their habits. Tens of thousands of people are killed, maimed, and injured by automobiles driven by drugged and drunken drivers each year. Add to this the heartache of parents whose offspring abuse drugs and the strong negative influence on siblings who "get turned on" by older, drug-abusing brothers and sisters.

Many youth and young adults charged with rape, assault, and murder have cited the influence of alcohol or drugs as a reason for these deeds. PCP, in particular, is most frequently associated with violent, senseless crimes. Despite widespread knowledge of its ability to cause unpredictable violent behavior, memory loss, and uncontrollable reactions, smoking PCP-laced cigarettes has become an accepted part of life for many inner-city teenagers. The half-crazed behavior seen in teens under this drug's influence has prompted some police departments to provide their officers with special training for dealing with PCP users.[12] Another drug responsible for robberies and violent crimes by desperate young addicts is a concentrated form of cocaine known on the streets as "crack" or "rock." Urban police forces are becoming increasingly alarmed by the extraordinary ability of crack, which is smoked rather than sniffed, to produce compulsive and violent behavior in those who use it.

The list of victims of drug and alcohol abuse is a long one. It includes the many thousands of disrupted American classrooms and teachers disillusioned by drug-abusing students who take time away from other students and resources away from the general school program. The most helpless victims, however, are the babies born to drug abusers. They risk having birth defects such as mental retardation, distorted facial features, and heart ailments. Such impairments have even been observed in babies of women who used large quantities of alcohol or tobacco during pregnancy and have been described by physicians as the "fetal alcohol syndrome" and the "fetal tobacco syndrome."[13]

Finally, the drug users themselves pay a price not always recognized until years later. For example, because of a crackdown on the chemicals previously used in making cocaine, drug traffickers are now processing the drug with benzene, a chemical known to cause leukemia and genetic damage in humans.[14]

## Drug Dependence

Dr. Robert DuPont, former head of the National Institute on Drug Abuse, and others [15] have identified three drugs—alcohol, marijuana, and cocaine—as requiring special attention since (1) they are used more frequently than any others and (2) they are the gateway to the use of all other drugs. "They are dangerous," he says, "because they are mistakenly thought to be harmless," and ". . . are likely to produce full-blown dependence partly because use of these drugs is widely—and wrongly—thought to be easily controlled." In general, the earlier drug use begins (under age 15), the heavier and more serious it will become.[16]

According to experts,[17] there are four steps to drug dependence—the physical or psychological compulsion to use a drug on a continuous basis:

1. Experimentation and first-time use, which even if unpleasant fails to discourage many adolescents. This occurs often, but not always, during the late grade school or early middle school/junior high years. Generally students experiment together with friends.
2. Occasional or "social" use, which is characterized by infrequent (usually less than once a week) acceptance of drugs offered by drug-abusing peers or older siblings often after an adolescent has been repeatedly exposed to drug-abusing peers and/or adults. This and the "regular use" stage usually occur during the late middle school/junior high and early senior high school years.
3. Regular use (typically once or twice a week), a stage during which the chosen drug is actively sought out and an attempt is made to maintain a personal supply of the substance. At this stage

extracurricular and sports involvements decrease, grades begin to drop, and students may begin to steal from parents and/or pilfer from others.

4. Dependence (or addiction), the final stage in a almost indispensable part of the user's life. At this stage solitary use increases and the student may find it difficult to face the day without drugs.

## Drug Use and Abuse

The problem with drug use—even experimentation—is that it can lead to dependence. And the problem with drug dependence, as discussed earlier in this chapter, is that not only can it have tragic consequences for the abuser, but it also impacts negatively on the rest of society as well.

For the purpose of research, "use" and "abuse" are distinguished from each other by social scientists. Others who make the distinction, however, often inadvertently condone occasional "social" use of various drugs, particularly alcohol and marijuana. While it is true that not everyone who experiments with drugs becomes dependent, it should be remembered that both of these drugs are generally illegal for teenagers to use and both carry serious health hazards.

No one becomes dependent on a drug overnight.* But some youngsters may progress directly from experimentation to regular use, just as some may never use drugs again after initial experimentation. It takes time, however, for a physical tolerance, the need for ever-increasing quantities of the drug to produce the same pleasurable experience, to be built up. I believe that any nonmedically prescribed use of a chemical substance to produce an artificially pleasurable experience by a child or ado-

*Some experts now think, however, that it may be possible to become addicted to "crack," going from experimentation all the way to dependency, in a very short period of time.

lescent constitutes drug abuse and has the potential to seriously harm and adversely affect that youngster's life.

## Street Terms

Drug abuse like any social phenomenon has its own vocabulary. Technical terms like "tolerance," "dependence," and "narcotic" are defined as they are used in the body of this book. Street terms, or slang, also are incorporated to the extent possible and useful. Since most adolescent drug abusers use street terms, some grasp of basic terminology will be helpful to readers. Keep in mind, however, that terminology may vary over time and from place to place.

ACID — LSD.

BLACK BEAUTIES / DEXIES / BENNIES — Stimulants (uppers) available in oral capsules, which may also be dissolved for injection.

BONG — A water or other kind of pipe for smoking marijuana.

BURNOUT — A person whose perceptions and emotions are deadened and apathetic from too much drug use—a "zombie."

BUZZ — Similar to a high or euphoric feeling when intoxicated as a result of taking drugs.

CLEAN — Not being in possession of, or not using, any drugs.

CRACK — A new, inexpensive purified form of cocaine ready to be smoked that comes as "rocks" in small plastic vials.

CRANK — Amphetamines.

DROPPING ACID — Ingesting LSD.

DRUGGIES / DOPERS — Young people who take drugs, as distinguished from "straight" kids or those who do not take drugs.

ECSTASY — Methylenedioxymethamphetamine (MDMA), a controversial drug that has properties similar to hallucinogens and amphetamines.

FREAK OUT — A panic reaction to taking LSD or other hallucinogenic drug.

FREE-BASE — Adding chemical solutions to cocaine in order to smoke it and rid it of impurities. The solution added to the cocaine is usually a highly flammable solvent that can cause serious accidents.

GARBAGE HEAD — Someone who will take anything to get high.

GET OFF — To achieve a "high" as a result of taking a drug.

GOOFBALL— A barbiturate or amphetamine pill.

GRASS — Marijuana.
POT
GANJA

GREEN— PCP; or marijuana soaked in PCP (lovely), and parsley soaked in PCP (green).
LOVE BOAT
BOAT
LOVELY

HEAD — A heavy user of drugs.

HEAVEN — Cocaine.
COKE
"C"

HIGH — A state of intoxication as a result of taking drugs.

HIT — A puff or a single dose of a drug.

JOINT — A marijuana cigarette.

NARC — To inform on or report a drug user to authorities.

NOD — A drowsy, dreamy dozing state following the taking of a drug, usually an opiate, due to its sedative effect.

O.D. — Overdose, usually taking an excessive amount of a drug with severe adverse physical and mental effects, sometimes death.

POPPERS — Amyl nitrate, a drug that usually comes in a vial that is broken in a handkerchief and inhaled; used to stimulate sexual experience.

REDS — Secobarbital, a short-acting barbiturate.
RED DEVILS

ROACH — The end or "butt" of a marijuana cigarette.

RUSH — The initial onset of a warm, orgasmlike feeling, a euphoria, and physical well-being immediately after a drug has been injected.

SKIN POPPING — To inject a drug subcutaneously. The onset of the drug is not so immediate as with "mainlining," injecting intravenously.

SNORT — To inhale usually cocaine or heroin through the nose.

SPACED OUT — Intoxication as a result of taking drugs, or a dulling of the senses as a result of prolonged psychoactive drug use.

SPEED — Amphetamines or other stimulants.

SPEEDBALL — A mixture of cocaine and heroin or amphetamines injected as a mixture.

STONED — A state of intoxication as a result of taking drugs.

STRAIGHT — A state of, or an individual, *not* using drugs.

TOKE — A puff of marijuana or other drug that is smoked.

TOOTER — A tube, often made from rolling a paper or dollar bill into a cylinder, used to snort or sniff cocaine from a flat surface into one's nose.

TRIP — To take a hallucinogenic drug.

TURN ON — To introduce someone to drugs; to be high on drugs.

WAKE UP — The first dose of drugs in the morning.

WASTED — A state of intoxication as a result of taking drugs.

YELLOW JACKETS — Pentobarbital, a short-acting barbiturate.

# Resources

## Student Drug Use

Baron, Jason D. *Kids and Drugs*. New York: Putnam Publishing Group, 1983.

Gold, Mark S. *800–Cocaine*. New York: Bantam Books, 1984.

Janeczek, Curtis L. *Marijuana, Time for a Closer Look*. Columbus, Ohio: Healthstar Publications, 1981.

Johnston, Lloyd D., and others. *Use of Licit and Illicit Drugs by American High School Students, 1975–1984*. Rockville, Md.: National Institute on Drug Abuse, 1985. (A single copy of this survey of high school seniors, which is updated annually, is free by writing NIDA, 5600 Fishers Lane, Rockville, MD 20857.)

McHenry, Patrick C., and others. "The Role of Drugs in Adolescent Suicide Attempts." *Suicide and Life-Threatening Behavior* 13, no. 3 (Fall 1983): 166–75.

Ruy, Lynda Y., and Johnson, Norbert. "Adolescent Suicide." *Personnel and Guidance Journal* 62, no. 3 (November 1983): 131–35.

Tessler, Diane Jane. *Drugs, Kids, and Schools*. Glenview, Ill.: Scott, Foresman and Co., 1980.

Also available from the National Institute on Drug Abuse (NIDA):

*Angel Dust in Four American Cities: An Ethnographic Study of PCP Users.*

*Cocaine Addiction—It Costs Too Much.*

*Drug Abuse in Rural America.*

*Drug Abuse Patterns Among Young Polydrug Users and Urban Appalachian Youths.*

*Heroin-Addicted Parents and Their Children.*

*Inhalants, The Deliberate Inhalation of Volatile Substances*, series 30, no. 2.

*Marijuana and Youth: Clinical Observations on Motivation and Learning.*

Research Issue 29, *Drugs and the Family.*

Research Monograph 38, *Drug Abuse and the American Adolescent.*

## Drugs and Their Effects

Allinson, Russel R. *Drug Abuse, Why It Happens and How to Prevent It.* Lower Burrell, Pa.: Valley Publications, 1984.

Baron, *Kids and Drugs.*

Cohen, Sidney. *The Substance Abuse Problem.* New York: Haworth Press, 1981.

Drug Information Flyer Series (available in English and Spanish), NIDA.

Drug Information Flyers, Phoenix House, 164 West 74th Street, New York, NY 10023.

Also available from NIDA:

*Phencyclidine: A Review.*

Research Monograph 31, *Marijuana Research Findings 1980.*

Research Monograph 44, *Marijuana Effects on the Endocrine and Reproduction System.*

## Terminology and General Information

Lingeman, Richard R. *Drugs from A to Z: A Dictionary.* 2d rev. ed. New York: McGraw-Hill, 1974.

*Cocaine Pain* (1984)
Produced by J. Gary Mitchell Film Co.
16 mm, 32 min.
MTI Teleprograms, Inc.
108 Wilnot Road
Deerfield, IL 60015
(800) 323-6301

This film uses candid interviews with participants in a "Cokenders" program to identify reasons behind the sudden rise in cocaine addiction. Although it is about adult cocaine users, the film is useful in teaching adolescents and young adults about long-term consequences.

The following films are available free by writing at least three weeks in advance to

Modern Talking Picture Service Scheduling Center
NIDA Free Loan Collection
5000 Park Street, North
St. Petersburg, FL 33709

(For emergency service—less than three weeks ahead—call (813) 541-5763.)

*For Parents Only: What Kids Think of Marijuana* (1980) 70366F, 70366U
Produced by Vision Associates for Drug Enforcement Administration
30 min., color
In 3/4" U-matic videocassette, and 16 mm film formats

In this documentary on adolescent use of marijuana, several teenagers—current and former users—discuss beliefs, thoughts, feelings, and fears. Parents also reveal their anxiety and search for solutions to marijuana problems. A psychiatrist addresses straightforward comments to parents, and two youth counselors offer fresh insights on marijuana use.

*Growing Up Stoned* (1984) 74156F
Produced by Dave Bell Associates, Inc.
51 min., color

Audience: General adult, parents groups, health professionals

This film presents portraits of three teenage heavy users of drugs and alcohol: Adam, 17; John, 15; and Heather, 16. It documents the disastrous effects of their drug use on themselves, their families, their schooling, and their communities, in interviews and as the episodes happened. When the film was made, the three youngsters had become drug free.

*The PCP Story* (1976) 70025F
Produced by Film Tree Productions
26 min., color

Audience: General, health professionals and paraprofessionals, law enforcement

This film explores the drug problem of PCP (phencyclidine) abuse. It presents facts about its effects, the people who use it, and those who are trying to help end the life-threatening emergencies caused by it.

*Pills and Alcohol (Sedatives)* (1979) 76377F
Produced by Post Time Print and Tape
25 min., color

Audience: General

Dr. Lawrence Wharton, a specialist in alcoholism and drug abuse, describes the sedatives, including alcohol, mild tranquilizers, barbiturates, "daytime sedatives," and bromides. Dr. Wharton discusses the length of action in the body of these drugs as well as their combined sedative-stimulant effect. He stresses that a user who loses control over any one of the sedatives cannot control any others.

*Pot* (1982) 70062F
Produced by Gary Whiteaker Company, Inc.
29 min., color

Audience: General, young adult

David Ohlms, M.D., discusses marijuana's effects on body systems. He describes the effects of THC, the active principle in marijuana, on the brain and the genital areas, then explores its possible effects on neurons and neurotransmitters. He discusses distorted perceptions related to marijuana, "flashbacks," and the amotivational syndrome (loss of ambitions and goals).

*Psychoactive* (1976) 70026F
Produced by William E. Cohen
29 min., color

Audience: Senior high, college, adult

This film classifies drugs into five families, such as stimulants and sedatives, and describes their effects on the body. Nine different major body systems are shown. Combining live action and animation, the film explains how the body systems function and how each drug may affect several systems. Vivid scenes show possible dangers.

*Reading, Writing and Reefer* (1978) 70339F and 70340F (two reels)
Produced by NBC News
52 min., color

Audience: General, parents

Edwin Newman narrates this documentary exploring the rapid increase in marijuana use by American youngsters. Two boys describe their marijuana use and its marked effects on their lives. Although children think marijuana harmless, evidence shows that smoking can irritate the lungs, may cause cancer, and can impair driving. The film shows the illegal smuggling network stretching from Colombia to the United States.

The following film is available from

FMS Productions, Inc.
P.O. Box 4428
5520 East Montecito Street
Santa Barbara, CA 93140

*Cocaine: The Highs and Lows* (1986)
28 min., 16 mm film or videocassette

This film explores the addiction process from beginning through treatment and recovery. Dr. Mark Gold's book, *800–Cocaine*, comes with it free.

CHAPTER 2

# Why Young People Take Drugs

It got to where the reason I was doing them was because I couldn't put them down.

—Anthony, age 17

No one can adequately explain why young people use drugs, although many people have tried. Before examining some of the explanations, let's hear from some students.

I was with my cousin once and she offered me a drag on a joint. I guess I was curious. Later, I started using speed, but I don't know why. I just liked it.

—Mary, age 15

I was always scared to smoke dope. But like the first time I tried it and nothing happened—I didn't die or freak out—the fear was gone.

—Jenny, age 16

I had a big problem going from elementary to junior high. I was fat and I had no friends. This kid in seventh grade offered me some dope to smoke during lunch. He was the only kid who'd talk to me. I'm not exactly sure what it was, but I really got high. After that I tried all sorts of stuff to get that same feeling.

—Paul, age 17

I did it because everyone else was doing it. I figured why not. Besides, that was the only place I got accepted . . . by the druggies. Then when my mom and dad got divorced, I really got into drugs. I was tired of feeling bad all the time because of my parents. Later when I was hustling, I used to get beat up a lot, so that's when I got into acid . . . to escape my problems.

—Stan, age 16

I first started drinking at dances and parties in junior high. When I went into high school, I wasn't a big man anymore. School became pretty boring for me, so I started doing pot, and went on up the ladder to coke and acid.

—Bob, age 17

> I don't know why I started using drugs. It just seemed like a good idea at the time. I guess there was nothing else to do.
>
> —Tracy, age 15
>
> I had no intention of using. I just wanted to try it.
>
> —Laurin, age 13

# Examining the Reasons

It has been said that if students only knew what they were letting themselves in for when they abuse drugs, none in his or her right mind would ever touch them. Knowledge, however, is not the same as wisdom. Consider how many people continue to smoke cigarettes although they know that it increases their chances of cancer and heart disease. Simply telling kids about the effects of drugs is not always enough to discourage them from trying them, particularly after they have reached a stage of development where they no longer accept what their teachers and parents say as gospel. Kids take drugs for a variety of reasons. The following sections examine some of them.

## Pleasure

One reason why young people take drugs is that drugs give pleasure; they make the user feel good. Chronic drug abusers seek to gain pleasure and avoid the pain of withdrawal. When people become dependent or addicted, these two factors can produce compunction. As the drug abuser builds up a physical tolerance to a particular drug, he or she requires greater and greater quantities to produce the same high, or pleasurable experience. Unlike most natural highs, such as the pleasure derived from performing well on an examination or playing one's best on a winning athletic team, the pleasure from taking drugs does not last. In fact, after the high ceases, the drug abuser usually experiences the opposite of pleasure—dullness, emptiness, and sometimes discomfort. Nor is there any feeling of contentment, accomplishment, or fulfillment. The desire to "feel good," often cited by adolescent drug abusers, points to the youngster's inability to derive pleasure in natural, more socially acceptable, and less harmful ways.

## Peer Pressure

The desire to be accepted by one's peers frequently becomes an important determiner of kids' behavior about the time they leave elementary and enter middle school/junior high. The statements of students given at the beginning of this chapter indicate the influence of friends and classmates, particularly when kids experiment and begin using drugs. Peer support of drug experimentation among adolescents, therefore, probably reflects the increasing importance of peer influence during this stage of development.

Most initial drug use takes place, researchers tell us, between the ages of 12 and 18.[18] Preoccupation with the opinions of others, acceptance by others, having friends, and being found attractive by the opposite sex, all are natural concerns of adolescents. But these concerns also make kids vulnerable. Those who are not emotionally strong may succumb to negative peer pressures, to the temptation of being welcomed to a new group of friends, friends who make few demands except to share their desire to use drugs. One research study[19] found that the best predictor of illicit adolescent drug use is the school climate. Student drug use is influenced by the amount of drugs used in a school, the prevalence of drug-using behavior, and the degree to which this behavior is accepted among the drug user's social clique. Indeed, several studies[20] indicate that association with drug-using peers (particularly close friends) during adolescence is one of the strongest predictors of adolescent drug use.

## Life Stress and Pain

For many youngsters, childhood and adolescence can be a painful period. Simply experiencing the natural changes in the body, the mind, and the emotions during adolescence can be difficult enough. Add to this new roles in school and at home, more responsibilities, emerging sexuality, and increased expectations to do well in school and get accepted to college or earn a scholarship, and it is easy to appreciate the tremendous pressure adolescents sometimes feel as they grow up. This pressure can come not only from peers but from teachers and parents as well.

Another source of stress is family dysfunction or simply not getting along with parents or siblings. Feeling misunderstood or unappreciated can result in unhappiness and depression. The inability to cope with stress and unhappiness, then, may lead some to seek escape from the pain of everyday living by taking drugs, running away, or even attempting suicide.

Youngsters who live in poverty as well as those who live in affluence can become unhappy and depressed. Those who are poor, however, may be subjected to additional stresses, such as poor living conditions, no job, no spending money. Minority and refugee youngsters often must cope with stress caused by discrimination, inability to speak English, and the frustration of trying to understand and function in a different and bewildering culture. Whether rich or poor, black or white, Asian or Hispanic, or American Indian, almost all adolescent drug abusers express a feeling of alienation,[21] of being out of place, of not belonging, of being estranged.

In the minds of impressionable, vulnerable adolescents, almost anything can become unbearably painful:

- Failure to make the team
- Being spurned by a member of the opposite sex
- Divorce or separation of parents

- Failing a subject, or even a single test
- Death of a parent or grandparent
- Moving up to middle school/junior high or high school and discovering that no friends are in any of their classes
- Moving to a new town and school away from friends
- Being left at home unsupervised by working parents
- Having an abusive or alcoholic parent.

The large numbers of immigrant and refugee students born outside the United States often must contend with additional stress factors, such as the following:

- Not knowing how to get help during a crisis
- Not being able to make friends among American students
- Feeling guilty about relatives or friends who died or were left behind
- Being left suddenly without the comfort and security of an extended family that consisted of parents, grandparents, uncles, and aunts
- Being expected to serve as the linguistic and cultural translator of this new U.S. society for their elders
- Being expected by parents to obey the customs and rules of their "old" society and by their teachers and classmates to obey the customs and rules of American society
- Having little or no previous schooling in their native country.

## Experimentation

Most developmental psychologists agree that curiosity and risk taking are vital to healthy human growth and development. This need to explore and test may lead a child or adolescent to experiment with drugs. Many who experiment do not continue using drugs. But for those who do experiment—for whatever innocent reasons—and then become heavier users, the results can be harmful to normal growth and development.

## Rebelliousness

In contrast with experimentation, researchers[22] have found that drug abuse, especially in early and mid-adolescence, is sometimes part of a general pattern of rebelliousness and nonconforming behavior. A wide array of personality traits, including nonconformity to traditional values, a high tolerance for deviance, resistance to traditional authority, a strong need for independence, and normlessness, have all been linked to drug use.[23] Many of these same traits are associated with antisocial and delinquent behavior, and often precede drug use.

## A Chemical Society

Everywhere they look—movies, TV, newspapers, home, and school—young people encounter drugs: ads for medicines to dull pain; beer commercials promising friends, success in athletics, and good times; rock videos and movies glorifying drug use; and almost daily media revelations that professional athletes and other role models use drugs. Society's ready acceptance of unprescribed drugs such as aspirin, alcohol, and caffeine pills are not lost on adolescents. They also note the truck driver who uses amphetamines to stay awake at the wheel and the housewife who needs barbiturates to get to sleep after a hectic day. The message is clear: "Everyone's doing it; you can, too."

Despite consistent findings[24] that young people are influenced to use drugs by the drug-using behaviors of adults, only recently have drug abuse prevention campaigns been geared to adults. Not only sports and entertainment celebrity role models, but parents themselves have a significant influence on their children's attitudes toward the use of drugs. Indeed, some studies[25] show that most parents of adolescents who are heavy drug users are themselves heavy users of illegal drugs and, often, alcohol. In general, whether or not an adolescent's parents abuse drugs, his or her use of drugs considered acceptable by the community—cigarettes, beer, or wine—will precede use of substances the community considers unacceptable.[26] According to some persons, regulations against any kind of drug use, including cigarettes and alcohol, therefore, should be enforced on school grounds; and stores in the community displaying drug paraphernalia and magazines should be closed "because they are an all too visible symbol of adult complacency toward adolescent drug use."[27]

## Low Self-Esteem and Poor Life Attitude

If all the previously listed factors are such strong incentives for young people to abuse drugs, why, readers might wonder, don't more kids use drugs? While most youngsters face many of these common pressures—stress, pain, and peer and societal influences—nonusers as a group seem to possess a stronger self-concept. Along with a relationship among drug use, school problems, and family dysfunction,[28] studies also have noted a relationship between low self-concept and drug use.

In a study of drug use among students in six Boston area school systems, Smith and Fogg[29] found that adolescents who used marijuana "did not feel capable, valued, and accepted." Conversely, Tessler, surveying junior high and high school nonusers in California, found that such youngsters regarded themselves as successful in school, reasonably attractive, and well-liked. Tessler[30] also found that while drug users often said that they used drugs because their friends were users, non-drug-using students claimed their own "self-respect" was more important than their friends' use of drugs.

A low opinion of self can be the result of external or self-generated factors. Whatever its genesis, feeling unattractive, dumb, not likable, incapable, unloved, and unworthy can turn the world into a dull, boring, unhappy place—a place where exerting the energy to meet life's challenges does not seem worthwhile, and where drugs offer a way out.

This apparent lack of any kind of motivation except to get high that so many "druggies" today exhibit may be their way of showing that they have no confidence in themselves. Others react to real or imagined rejection, abuse, and attacks to their egos with counterattacks on parents, teachers, and other authority figures. Such counterattacks can take the form of vandalism, truancy, shoplifting, and drug abuse. Some research has shown a definite relationship between drug abuse and all these offenses, as well as poor school performance.[31]

## Family Influences

In addition to parental drug-using behavior and attitudes toward drugs, the quality of parent-child interactions is also related to a child's use or nonuse of drugs. In particular, the following characteristics were observed to be common to families of drug-abusing adolescents:

- Negative communication patterns, such as frequent criticism, blaming, and lack of praise
- Inconsistent and unclear behavior limits
- Denial of the child's drug use
- Unrealistic parental expectations
- Family self-medication
- Miscarried expressions of anger.[32]

## School Factors

We do not know whether poor performance in school causes drug use among students. Certainly it commonly follows the onset of regular drug use; and drug users appear to perform more poorly in middle school/junior high and senior high school than do nonusers.[33] Some researchers have sought to show that first grade teachers' ratings of antisocial behavior can be used as predictors of later drug abuse.[34] Whether or not this is valid, it is a fact that students not committed to educational pursuits are more likely to engage in drug use.[35]

The annual survey of American high school seniors by University of Michigan researchers shows consistently that the use of hallucinogens, cocaine, heroin, stimulants, sedatives, or tranquilizers is significantly lower among students planning to attend college; and that drug users tend to be absent, cut more classes, and generally perform more poorly than nonusers.[36] Clearly, what goes on at school has a great deal to do with why kids take drugs; and the fact that they do take drugs has a great deal to do with what goes on at school.

## So What?

Besides all the foregoing reasons for drug abuse among young people, researchers have posited scores of others from "to find out more about one's self" to "to improve sex." Most credible reasons, however, probably can be subsumed under the general headings used in this chapter. Nevertheless, the question remains, why should anyone care why kids take drugs? Some people take the position that regardless of the reasons they take them, no real help can be given to drug abusers until they stop using them, and that preoccupation with underlying psychological and sociological factors only will serve as a diversion from the task at hand—getting drug-abusing youngsters to stop and preventing potential users from starting.

Proponents of this view feel that schools and parents have been too lenient, that they must take a firmer stance to forbid drug use, and to punish transgressors. Others have pointed out, however, that understanding why kids abuse drugs will help prevent as well as stop their use. Both views seem to have merit; using both approaches may therefore make the most sense.

# Resources

## Why Kids Take Drugs

*Adolescent Peer Pressure: Theory, Correlates, and Programs: Implications for Drug Abuse Prevention.* Rockville, Md.: National Institute on Drug Abuse, 1981.

Committee on Ways and Means, U.S. House of Representatives. *Children in Poverty.* May 22, 1985. Congressional Research Service and the Congressional Budget Office. Washington, D.C.: U.S. Government Printing Office, 1985.

Jones, Coryl LaRue, and Battjes, Robert J., eds. *Etiology of Drug Abuse: Implications for Prevention.* Rockville, Md.: National Institute on Drug Abuse, 1985.

Rumbaut, R. D., and Rumbaut, R. G. "The Family in Exile: Cuban Expatriates in the United States." *American Journal of Psychiatry* 133 (1976): 395–99.

Williams, C., and Westermeyer, J. "Psychiatric Problems Among Adolescent Southeast Asian Refugees." *Journal of Nervous and Mental Disease* 171 (1983): 79–85.

Williams, C., and Westermeyer, J. *Refugees and Mental Health.* New York: Hemisphere Publishing Co., 1986.

The following films are available free from the Modern Talking Picture Service Scheduling Center (see address and directions at the end of Chapter 1):

*Alcohol, Drugs . . . A Way Out* (1976) 70323F
Produced by Sandler Institutional Films, Inc.
20 min., color

Audience: High school through adults; parents; particularly current heavy users of alcohol or drugs

The narrator challenges viewers by asking about their attitudes toward drug-taking, and suggesting that some attitudes indicate trouble ahead. Two actors, portraying heavy users, voice their evasions;

the narrator helps them begin to take constructive steps in their lives. A segment called "The Winner's Game" shows how to overcome fears of insecurity and change.

*Alcohol and Drugs . . . Making the Decision* (1978) 70360F
Produced by Sandler Institutional Films, Inc.
36 min., color

Audience: Middle school/junior high through adults, parents

Paul Williams and Meredith Baxter Birney show the issues involved in making decisions about alcohol and other drugs. Actors demonstrate how some youngsters blame others for their problems while nonactors tell their success in overcoming their own drug problems. Ms. Birney discusses how to fight fears and how to arrive at decisions. The narrators stress, "There are no short cuts to feeling good."

*Alcohol, Drugs or Alternatives* (1973) 70282F
Produced by Sandler Institutional Films, Inc.
25 min., color

Audience: Senior high school and young adult

This film shows how young people may attempt to deal with insecurity and inadequacy by taking drugs. Christopher George and Tommy Smothers demonstrate that a young person can make the difficult effort to acknowledge and overcome destructive feelings. The film stresses that young people can help one another, and that satisfying alternatives to drug use exist.

*Almost Everybody Does* (1970) 70041F
Produced by Wombat Productions
14 min., color

Audience: Upper elementary; general

Emphasizing that all people have good and bad feelings, this film focuses on how people learn to cope with these feelings. Scenes from an average middle-class family give examples of coping—relaxing with a martini, smoking, chatting, or taking an occasional pill. The film asks, "When does a drug that changes the way a person feels become harmful or dangerous?"

*Can a Parent Be Human?* (1971) 70311F
Produced by Dimension Films. Part of "The Searching Years" series
11½ min., color

Audience: High school, parents

This film explores the question "How can parents reach their children better?" In a spontaneous, intense discussion, young people compare ways in which parents frighten children with ways in which they make successful contact. After a break for class comments and activity, the film continues with a role play in which a distant father attempts to come closer to his son.

*We Have an Addict in the House* (1972) 70308F
Produced by Communications Foundation, Inc.
30 min., color

Audience: Youth, parents, general adults

In alternating sequences, teenagers talk about why they used drugs, their alienation from their parents, and their strong need to belong to a group. In turn, their parents recount their shock at their youngsters' addiction and their pain as they confront the reality of their family situation. As the dialogues proceed, the parents and teenagers gradually achieve understanding and reconciliation with one another.

*Soft Is the Heart of a Child* and *Lots of Kids Like Us.* These two films (30 min. each) are available from Gerald T. Rogers Productions, 5225 Old Orchard Road, Suite 23, Skokie, IL 60077.

*Soft Is the Heart of a Child* depicts the struggle of a family to stay together under the stress of an alcoholic father. A school counselor attempts to help the children and their parents. The second film, *Lots of Kids Like Us*, deals with a similar theme.

*Calling the Shots: The Advertising of Alcohol* (1986, 30 min.) is available in 16 mm film or videocassette from Cambridge Documentary Films, Inc., P.O. Box 385, Cambridge, MA 02139, (617) 354–3677.

This high school and college-level film examines the images used by advertisers to sell alcohol. It analyzes how the fears and needs of young people are used to create the new young alcohol consumer; and it demonstrates how some advertising deliberately disguises the warning signs of problem drinking and falsely links alcohol with those qualities—happiness, success, sexual fulfillment, prestige, athletic ability, creativity—that its abuse diminishes and destroys.

## Child Growth and Development

Anderson, Joan Webster. *Teen Is a Four Letter Word (A Survival Kit for Parents*). White Hall, Va.: Betterway Publications, 1983.

Brenton, Myron. *How to Survive Your Child's Rebellious Teens.* New York: Bantam Press, 1981.

Cretcher, Dorothy. *Steering Clear: Helping Your Child Through the High-Risk Drug Years.* Oak Grove, Minn.: Winston Press, 1982.

Elkind, David. *All Grown Up and No Place to Go: Teenagers in Crisis.* Reading, Mass.: Addison-Wesley, 1984.

Fornaciari, Suzanne. *How to Talk to Kids About Drugs.* Washington, D.C.: Potomac Press, 1980.

Meyer, Roberta. *The Parent Connection: How to Communicate with Your Child About Alcohol and Other Drugs.* New York: Franklin Watts, 1984.

Novello, Joseph R. *Bringing Up Kids American Style.* New York: A and W Publishers, 1981.

CHAPTER 3

# Whose Problem Is It?

Whatever class I was in while I was high, the information went right through my head. I wasn't paying attention at all.

—David, age 16

I'd smoke a couple of bolts before I'd leave the house, catch a ride with a friend, and do some on the way to school. We'd meet up in the smoking area and just not go to first period if we knew where we could get some. When I went to class I was so strong I didn't want to do any work. I would crash out and sleep, or just raise hell.

—Frank, age 17

Before a problem can be solved, someone must take the responsibility for dealing with it. Who should take responsibility for dealing with drug and alcohol abuse among children and youth? Whose problem is it? Is it a school problem? Is it a police or public health issue that should be addressed by the government? Clearly, the problem belongs to all of us who are affected by it—schools, parents, students, and society. In sum, it is the community-at-large that is affected by drug abuse; and all segments of the community, including the schools, must become involved in dealing with it.

## Why Drug Abuse Is a School Problem

"Why is it that the school is expected to solve all of society's problems? Teenage pregnancy, suicide, drug abuse, poor nutrition, low self-esteem—you name it and we're supposed to cure it. Well, I don't know about you, but I was hired to teach algebra, not to play at being a psychiatrist." Sound familiar? It is a legitimate question. Why should teachers be expected to deal with these problems? What have such problems to do with teaching algebra or any other subject? The short answer to this question is they have everything to do with teaching. First of all, teenage pregnancy, suicide, low self-esteem, poor nutrition, and drug abuse may indeed be different facets of the same set of problems that are closely related to each other and to such other problems as class cutting, truancy, and disruptive behavior. If students are unavailable for instruction, either physically or mentally, teachers cannot teach them.

Moreover, the negative effect that one or two students nodding off or giggling at the back of the room can have on the rest of the class and on the teacher's attitude toward the class should not be overlooked. Certainly parents have primary responsibility for dealing with adolescent drug abuse, but without the active involvement of schools, the chances of successfully combating the problem are considerably reduced. Consider that (1) virtually all children and youth in the United States attend school, (2) many students spend more waking hours each weekday in contact with teachers than with their own parents, (3) schools have a profound effect on the outlooks and attitudes of young people, and (4) schools traditionally are concerned with the character as well as the cognitive and physical development of their students.

"All this may be true," one might argue, "but aren't we opening a Pandora's box of extra responsibility, work, and trouble for ourselves? What if the student I report retaliates by scratching up my car, or calling my home in the middle of the night? What if my principal gets the idea that I can't control my class? What if the student's family sues me for making accusations I can't prove?"

Yes, these are possible consequences, but their probability is low and the stakes are high. Yes, there may be authorities who do not want to acknowledge that a problem exists. But when a drug- or alcohol-connected student death or other tragedy occurs, the school board will want to know why someone did not try to head off the problem. More importantly, teachers need to become involved because the very lives of their students may be at stake and the viability of the schools' mission to prepare young people to be responsible for themselves and to gain the skills necessary to improve the quality of their lives and contribute to society does hang in the balance. Teachers cannot help but be involved.

## The Parent Movement

The major responsibility for dealing with adolescent drug abuse, of course, belongs to the parents. All over the country parents are banding together to combat drug and alcohol abuse. During the last half dozen years they have developed major initiatives at both national and local levels. Groups like PRIDE (Parents' Resource Institute for Drug Education), MADD (Mothers Against Drunk Driving), and the National Federation of Parents for Drug-Free Youth have lobbied successfully in many instances for enforcing existing laws, raising the legal drinking age to 21, and enacting tougher laws against advertising and selling drug paraphernalia. The interest of the White House in the problem also has lent impetus and strength to the movement. At the local level, such groups often push for tougher school regulations and policies against drug/alcohol use, training programs for parents, treatment programs for kids, and vigorous drug prevention campaigns in and outside the schools. The parent movement today has built up a head of steam. Many hard-fought political battles have made these groups sophisticated and assertive. Parents can be effective allies and supporters of school personnel interested in combating drug and alcohol abuse. They can help run political interference, help supply resources, and play the all-important cooperative role at home in providing consistency in rules and outlook.

## Students

Some of the school's most potentially powerful allies are drug-free students who increasingly are willing to fight against drug abuse among their peers. Non-drug-abusing students do not enjoy sitting in class with someone nodding off in the next seat, or entering lavatories where marijuana smoke accosts their senses, or being approached in the corridor or outside the school by druggies soliciting money for a hit, or being put in the uncomfortable position of going against pressure by peers to use drugs. Most of all, students are concerned about the deaths of classmates from drunk driving, suicides, and overdoses. Drug and alcohol abuse, therefore, is very much a problem for students whether or not they themselves use drugs.

Annual surveys of high school seniors by the University of Michigan have indicated that students have become more conservative in their views regarding drug use. Thirty-two percent of high school seniors favored legalization of marijuana in 1979, for example. That percentage dropped sharply to 19 percent in 1984.[37]

The importance of changing student attitudes, in breaking down existing norms, cannot be overestimated. The great majority of high school seniors now have friends who do not approve of using illegal drugs. More and more of these students are willing to risk being labeled "nerds," "outs," or "unpopulars." They are willing to speak out against drug and alcohol abuse at their schools. Teachers and other school personnel should encourage and assist this new development. In the coalition to combat drug and alcohol abuse, students are now ready to take their place. They can act as peer counselors, they can lobby against drug and alcohol abuse, and they can work to change the norms regarding teen drug and alcohol use in their school community. Experience has shown, however, that ongoing faculty support and encouragement are vital to sustain effective student activism in this area.

## Government and Community Agencies

Government and community agencies also are important allies. Some, such as police and health departments, tend to provide direct but narrow services because of their view of their missions. Most drugs of abuse are illegal. Therefore the enforcement role of police departments should be clear-cut. But often it is not. District attorneys may be hesitant to prosecute juvenile offenders. Juvenile judges' case loads may be backlogged, thus making enforcement uneven or, at worst, neglected. This is an area where parent groups can help by calling for tougher laws, harsher penalties, and stricter enforcement. Likewise, school/police/court liaisons must be set up to ensure consistent and coordinated treatment of particular offenses.

Ongoing interagency contact and cooperation also are important in order to avoid turf wars, or arguments between schools and government over respective areas of responsibility. Health and social service departments, for example, may consider drug treatment and rehabilitation programs to be their domain and question the schools' dabbling in these areas. Schools often are quite happy to leave this area of responsibility to those departments. Nevertheless, some notable successes in cooperative and joint responsibility in prevention, enforcement, and treatment of drug abuse problems do exist among schools and government/community agencies.

## Business

Business is concerned about student drug abuse and is willing to assume its share of the responsibility. For example, when the National Federation of Parents for Drug-Free Youth launched an ambitious youth training project (REACH America) to prepare young people to participate in drug prevention activities at school and in the community, the Metropolitan Life Insurance Foundation helped fund the effort.

When the Education Commission of the States asked several business leaders to advise the group on the subject of education, the resulting report reflected the private sector's concern that millions of teenagers are "disconnected" from society as a result of drug abuse, delinquency, pregnancy, and other related problems. Unlike *Nation at Risk* and other recent exhortations to the schools to raise academic standards and individual achievement, the business report *Action for Excellence* calls for schools not to neglect unmet social and human needs that may be adversely affecting up to half the high school population in some major U.S. cities. Again, the message is clear: business has a stake in what goes on in society and especially in the schools, and it is willing to help.

The nature of business concern with combating drug and alcohol abuse among the nation's youth is reflected in the news that hundreds of companies are setting up programs to combat drug abuse among their own employees. "Illegal drugs," says *Time* Magazine, "have become so pervasive in the U.S. workplace that they are used in almost every industry, the daily companions of blue and white collar workers alike."[38] Because the problem seems to be most prevalent among younger workers and because it costs them so much in lost productivity and health insurance, out of pure self-interest business is anxious to help stop it before it starts.

How can educators tap this source of help for their school? They can do what others do. Ask the local Lions Club to reprint antidrug brochures for general distribution. Ask the Chamber of Commerce to establish a teen drug abuse prevention committee to assist school and community efforts. Seek funding for school projects from local or regional corporations. In short, unashamedly ask the business community for help, and point to what so many other businesses are doing throughout the country.

## Building Coalitions

Classroom teachers, counselors, administrators, or other school employees need not, nor should they, work alone. They can reach out to form coalitions—with colleagues at school, with parents, with community agencies and private businesses, and with students. All that is required is a common acknowledgment that drug abuse is a problem that cannot be allowed to exist, that it can be dealt with effectively if all segments of the community are willing to work together. Each segment has something appropriate and useful to contribute. The following chapters discuss what the school's contribution is and how it can be made.

## Resources

### Who Is Affected

*Alcohol and Your Unborn Baby.* NIDA. Washington, D.C.: Superintendent of Documents, U.S. Government Printing Office, n.d.

Blume, Sheila. *Drinking and Pregnancy: Preventing Fetal Alcohol Syndrome.* Minneapolis: Johnson Institute, n.d. (20-page pamphlet available from Johnson Institute, 510 First Avenue, North, Minneapolis, MN 55403-1607, 1–800–231–5165)

Franks, Lucinda. "A New Attack on Alcoholism." *New York Times Magazine*, October 20, 1985.

Manatt, Marsha. *Parents, Peers, and Pot.* NIDA. Washington, D.C.: Superintendent of Documents, U.S. Government Printing Office, 1979.

Task Force on Education for Economic Growth. *Action for Excellence: A Comprehensive Plan to Improve Our Nation's Schools.* Denver, Colo.: Education Commission of the States, 1983. (This report was chaired by the governors of North Carolina and Delaware and the chairman of the Executive Committee of IBM.)

"Young Children of Alcoholics Target of Prevention Program." *ADAMHA NEWS* 10, no. 1, January 1984.

## Community Activities

Crowley, James F. *Alliance for Change: A Plan for Community Action on Adolescent Drug Abuse.* Minneapolis: Community Intervention, 1984.

Manatt, Marsha. *Parents, Peers, and Pot II.* NIDA. Washington, D.C.: Superintendent of Public Documents, U.S. Government Printing Office, 1983.

Task Force on Education for Economic Growth. *Action for Excellence: A Comprehensive Plan to Improve Our Nation's Schools.* Denver, Colo.: Education Commission of the States, 1983.

## Community Resources

Local affiliates of the following service organizations may have information and materials available on community efforts and drugs and alcohol:

Benevolent and Protective Order of Elks (active in Michigan on behalf of children of alcoholics)

Junior League (has an active community service component; local groups may be involved with local government and private education and prevention efforts)

Kiwanis Clubs

League of Women Voters (materials provide information on local laws and legislation dealing with drugs and alcohol)

Lions Clubs (have a very active drug and alcohol awareness program with booklets such as *Dead at Seventeen, PCP, Kids and Drugs,* and *The Battle Against Pot*, among others)

Local insurance companies may be able to provide brochures produced by some of the large national companies, or write directly to the following:

Advocacy Programs Division
Allstate Insurance Company
Allstate Plaza North F–3
Northbrook, IL 60062
(312) 291–5624
(*The Drunk Driver May Kill You*)

Blue Cross/Blue Shield
Public Relations
550 12th Street, N.W.
Washington, D.C. 20004
(*Think Before You Drink*, pamphlet on drinking and driving; *It's Up to You—What Parents Should Know and Do About Drug and Alcohol Abuse Among Children*, booklet about substance abuse for parents)

GEICO
GEICO Plaza
5260 Western Avenue
Washington, D.C. 20076
(*There's a Killer Loose*, pamphlet on drunk driving; *Teens, Alcohol, Other Drugs and Driving—A Guide for Parents*)

Other local resources to check with for information about what is happening in the community include the following:

Hospitals and other treatment centers or clinics
Mental health associations
Public health departments
Police community relations officers
Churches, synagogues, and other religious institutions with active community programs
Chambers of Commerce

## Parent Programs/Activities

Mothers Against Drunk Driving (MADD)
669 Airport Freeway, Suite 310
Hurst, TX 76053
(817) 268–MADD

Parents' Resource Institute for Drug Education (PRIDE)
100 Edgewood Avenue, Suite 1216
Atlanta, GA 30303
800–241–7946
(404) 658–2548

National Federation of Parents for Drug-Free Youth
8730 Georgia Avenue, Suite 200
Silver Spring, MD 20910
(301) 585–KIDS

The National PTA
700 North Rush Street
Chicago, IL 60611

## Student Groups

Students Against Driving Drunk (SADD)
c/o Robert Anastos
66 Diana Drive
Marlboro, MA 01752
(617) 481–3568

CHAPTER 4

# Recognizing the Problem

> I think my mom knew because it was obvious. I always came home and I'd barely speak to her. I didn't know what I was saying half the time. But she just pretended she didn't know. My teachers always knew—I knew they knew. But even if they had said something, I would deny it and lie and swear I'm not.
>
> —Janet, age 15

Adolescence, the period when most juvenile substance abuse occurs, is a period of turbulence, rapid growth, and change. Adolescents often behave strangely. How can school staff know, then, if a student is abusing drugs? A good knowledge of human growth and development, particularly for the age group concerned, is essential. Depending on the severity of the student's abuse, certain telltale signs may become apparent.

## Symptoms

The following are some basic questions school employees should ask themselves when they are concerned that an individual student may be abusing drugs:

1. Does the student have problems at school—truancy, class cutting, declining grades?
2. Is the student less interested in classroom and/or extracurricular activities?
3. Has the student been dropping old friends or been hanging out with new ones? Does the student hang around with known or suspected drug users?

4. Has the student's personality changed noticeably? Are there unexpected mood swings?
5. Does the student exhibit unprovoked hostility or frequently get into fights or vehement arguments?
6. Has the student become less responsible, exhibiting changed work habits—not doing homework, not turning in reports on time or doing them sloppily, showing up late for class?
7. Has the student's reputation gone downhill with friends, classmates, and teachers?
8. Has the student been involved with the law? (Some of the same problems associated with disruptive behavior—fights, extorting money from other students, vandalism—may also be responsible for students' taking drugs. As a rule of thumb, therefore, when you see a student who is in trouble, look for other signs that may indicate drug or alcohol abuse. One sign, however, does not *always* mean that such abuse is occurring.)
9. Does the student vehemently defend the right to drink or get high?
10. Does the student protest too much? Does the student resist talking or hearing about alcohol or drug abuse?
11. When talk of drugs occurs in class, does the student exchange knowing glances with others, giggling or laughing as if sharing a private joke?
12. Has the student's appearance changed dramatically: complexion worsened, hair dirty and unkempt, clothes slovenly? Has he or she gained or lost weight?
13. Does the student wear drug slogans or symbols on shirts, belt buckles, or other articles of clothing?
14. Do the student's notebooks, book covers, texts, or yearbook reflect drug-related information or doodling?

15. Does the student exhibit obvious signs of drug or alcohol use, such as bottles, bongs, or paraphernalia?
16. Do you detect visible or other signs about the student, such as a change in the size of the pupils of the eyes, hyperactivity or sluggishness, strange smells on the breath or clothing, slurred or incoherent speech?
17. Is the student always tired? Does the student tend to want to put his/her head on the desk and sleep at the back of the room, or nod off during class?
18. Has the student's physical health deteriorated? Is she/he pale or anemic-looking? Does she/he sniffle or cough a great deal? (Sleeping and eating patterns may be affected.)
19. To your knowledge has the student's relationship with members of his or her family deteriorated? Is the student withdrawn from the family, staying in his/her room and coming out only to eat or answer the telephone?
20. Does the student appear to be in a trance? (This last and extreme manifestation of excessive drug use over a prolonged period of time is sometimes referred to as "burnout." Long before burnout occurs, however, the more subtle symptoms should become apparent.)

## Denial

Parents are in a much better position than teachers to judge many of these behaviors. But they may not recognize the signs. They may work and the student may work, and they may spend very little time with each other. Indeed, teachers may have more contact with an adolescent who is abusing drugs and experiencing problems than the parents. Even if the parents do notice the child's strange behavior, they may not be able to admit to themselves that their child could be involved with drugs.

Occasionally parents may become angry with others for bringing this possibility to their attention. This phenomenon is called "denial"; it can be found not only among parents but among students and teachers as well. In fact, denial can be a real impediment to recognizing and acting upon drug abuse symptoms in young people. Sometimes because of denial, people simply do not bother to look for symptoms; and if they do notice them, they rationalize them away.

In some cases, teachers may be hesitant to "get a kid in trouble," particularly if the student is likable, has not caused any trouble, or is an important member of a team or club the teacher coaches or advises. Part of this phenomenon may stem from society's tendency to view drug abuse as a moral issue rather than as a disease. If a student had a compound fracture of the arm, however, teachers would not hesitate to get the youngster to a hospital, willingly or not. Drug abuse should be considered in the same way—as an ailment for which the afflicted person may not want treatment.

## Telltale Signs

Education staff who have a general concern that a student might be abusing drugs or alcohol should look for further evidence. The following are some additional signs suggested by professional drug and alcohol counselors:

1. *Redness Around the Eyes.* The harshness of marijuana smoke can irritate the skin and the eyes. Users may wear sunglasses, stay in dimly lit rooms, or use eye drops to try to cover this up. Teachers who have students in classes immediately after lunch, or after students have had opportunities to leave the building or stay unattended in lavatories or stairwells, should be particularly vigilant for these signs.
2. *Burns.* Students may exhibit burn marks on the thumb and index fingers and on the fingernails if they hold the marijuana roach, or cigarette, with

their fingers while trying to smoke it to the very end.

3. *Particles of Drugs.* Particles of drugs often stick between or on the teeth, or on the clothing, or protrude from the pockets of students who handle them.
4. *Matches and Ashes.* Marijuana is hard to keep lit. As a result, users often carry large numbers of matches with them and may exhibit small white ashes on their clothing.
5. *Odors.* Students may smell excessively, not of strange smoke but of deodorant or aftershave lotion. Often they will spray themselves, or the area or room they have been using, to cover the odor of drugs.
6. *Oral Hygiene.* Frequent brushing of teeth, gargling, or use of breath fresheners or mints may also be an attempt to remove unpleasant tastes and to disguise telltale odors from drugs.
7. *Unexplained Illnesses.* Students may develop a generally drowsy appearance, become tired and say they do not feel well but do not know why. School nurses should be on the lookout for such students, who frequently will not want to see the nurse. Those who abuse drugs and alcohol are usually more susceptible to illnesses such as frequent colds, vomiting, and dizziness.
8. *Feelings.* Students may begin to hide their feelings, which may result in emotional outbursts.

Once concern is aroused, it may be helpful to consult a checklist of factors that may shed additional light on the probability that a youngster is using drugs. For example, if some physical signs have been observed, try to determine how many of the following additional factors may be influencing the student's behavior:

1. *Organic*–Is there a known drug or alcohol abuse problem in the student's family that may suggest a predisposition to the problem?

2. *Affective*—Does the student exhibit—
   - low self esteem?
   - isolation?
   - impulsiveness?
   - negative feelings about school?
   - poor cognitive development?
3. *Behavioral*—Does the student exhibit—
   - poor self-discipline?
   - antisocial behavior?
   - poor judgment in the selection of friends?
   - uninvolvement with extracurricular activities?
4. *Social*—Does the student appear to be—
   - in conflict with what is socially acceptable?
   - unduly influenced by peers?
   - a member of a disorganized and/or dysfunctional family?
   - influenced by poor role models?

Drug therapists often make use of checklists containing hundreds of items in order to determine if and to what extent youngsters may be abusing drugs. The preceding list is a crude form of such an assessment tool. Most of the items given may be precursors of not only drug abuse but also of delinquency, suicide, eating disorders, sexual promiscuity, or other self-destructive behaviors. Any school employee who observes a student exhibiting a combination of several of these factors plus symptoms and telltale signs mentioned earlier in this chapter may be dealing with a very troubled youngster.

It is important to remember that none of these symptoms definitely means that students are using drugs. Adolescents can exhibit various forms of strange behavior without being on drugs. But when teachers feel strongly that one of their students may be abusing drugs, they should be prepared to do something about it. Many students in drug rehabilitation programs have described to me instances of coming to school drunk or getting high in school and simply nodding off at the back of the classroom with no one bothering them. These youngsters were sure that their teachers knew they were under the influence of drugs but ignored their condition because they did not care or did not want to become involved.

Teachers may be unsure, if they do suspect drugs, about what, if anything, they should do. They and all other school employees who suspect that a student may be abusing drugs are obligated, if not legally, then certainly ethically and professionally, to do something about it. The question is, what should they do? Chapter 5 discusses their role in the intervention process as well as other ways in which they can combat drug and alcohol abuse.

## Resources

*Adolescence and Depression,* National Institute on Mental Health. Washington, D.C.: Superintendent of Public Documents, U.S. Government Printing Office, 1984. Stock No. 017–024–01237–8, ADM 84–1337. (A packet of simply stated, nontechnical informational material about adolescent conflicts and their relationship to depression and suicide)

*How Can I Tell If My Child Is Using Drugs?* Parents' Resource Institute for Drug Education (PRIDE), 100 Edgewood Avenue, Suite 1216, Atlanta, GA 30303 (800–241–7946 or 404–658–2548)

Miller, Mary S. *Child Stress: Understanding and Answering Stress Signals of Infants, Children, and Teenagers*. Garden City, N.Y.: Doubleday and Co., 1982.

Schwartz, Richard H. "Frequent Marijuana Use in Adolescence: What Are the Signs, Stages?" *NASSP Bulletin* 69 (1985): 103–8.

# CHAPTER 5

# Attacking the Problem

> I had one teacher . . . she really deep-down cared about me. She knew I was getting high and she asked me about it. I was very upset. But she's the only person during my using that I ever apologized to because I realized this is the first person who has ever really cared about me. She's the one that got me to thinking. I backed off for a little while. But it got worse because everything seemed to pile up when I wasn't using.
>
> —Loretta, age 16

Successfully combating drug and alcohol abuse in a school requires that a number of pieces fit into place. The school administration and faculty must acknowledge that a problem may exist. The entire staff should understand the deleterious effects of drugs and alcohol on the students and on the school. The entire staff also should be familiar with the symptoms of drug and alcohol abuse, and be willing, within the appropriate limits of their roles, to become involved in helping kids in trouble.

## The Role of the Teacher

When confronted with student drug and alcohol use, most teachers are not sure what they can or should do. Often they feel powerless and alone. As a result, they may do nothing. They may ignore students who do not disrupt the class or remove from class those who are boisterous or unruly—neither of which may be an effective course of action. There are, however, some very specific steps that teachers should take in dealing with student drug use. They should—

1. Express their concerns to the student.
2. Notify the parents of their concerns.

3. Consult with and/or refer to appropriate staff.
4. Participate as appropriate in the intervention plan.

## Talking to the Student

While the responsibility for combating drug abuse in the school should be shared among administators, counselors, and teachers, it is the teacher who, because of daily contact with students, will generally come up against the problem first. When a student's symptomatic behavior arouses the teacher's concern, the first step should be to talk to the student, express concern, and offer help: "I'm really worried about you, John. Your behavior seems different. Would you like to talk about what's going on? Have you been getting high? You know, if you'd like to get some help, I'd be willing to work with you or to put you in touch with people who can help." In the absence of a trusting relationship, do not be surprised if the student initially reacts by denying that anything is wrong. Never initiate such a discussion, however, if the student appears to be under the influence of drugs or alcohol. The telltale signs, other than those of alcohol intoxication, are glazed eyes, extreme lethargy, sleepiness, or extremes in mood such as giggling, crying, and hostility. Depending on the school's policy, such students should be sent directly to the health room or office. When you next see the youngster be sure, however, to express concern and offer help. Do not simply assume someone else will take care of the problem or has done so. Check with the office or health room to see what, if any, followup has occurred.

Teachers who are not comfortable about asking if the student is taking drugs should simply express concern over the noted behavior and tell the student they are ready to help. Subsequently, however, they should be prepared to bring up the question of drug use, especially if the behavior continues or worsens. Avoiding the topic does no one any good. In fact, it may encourage the drug taking since silence enables the youngster to continue abusing drugs without being hassled. In this way, teachers, as well as parents and friends, may unwittingly contribute to the student's drug problem.

When working with students from other cultures, particularly limited-English-speaking refugees, be sensitive to and aware of cross-cultural differences in communication and interpersonal behavior. In general, follow this advice:

- Use a bilingual staff person whenever available to check the cultural appropriateness of your approach.
- Give students time to build trust before making a direct appeal to them or their parents.
- Be aware of the need of some students (particularly Southeast Asian refugees) for more formal structure and one-to-one interaction with authority figures.
- Do not interpret refugee students' "shyness" as dishonesty or resistance to authority.
- Do not allow the student to play the school off against the parent.
- Make sure that students do not become dependent on you and that they can take ownership for their own decisions.

## Talking to Parents

A second important step is to talk to parents. Here again, teachers may be troubled by the prospect of bearing bad news or making an accusation without being certain of its accuracy. Just as with the student, however, it is important to remember to express concern, not accuse, and offer to help, not threaten. Likewise, teachers may not wish to mention drug involvement initially unless the student's condition is extreme and obvious, but they certainly should mention it soon if the behavior persists. At first, it may be enough to express concern, describe the behavior, and inquire if the parent has noticed it too. A suggestion to consult a physician or counselor might also be made. Of course, the teacher need not always be the one who contacts the parents. Counselors and administrators can and should do so as well. In some schools, they may prefer to do so. But contact must be made, and frequently the parent will want to speak with the teacher who observed the behavior.

Remember, even if parents resist the initial offers of help and expressions of concern, the effort must be made and made again. Nor should teachers be deterred because of fear about legal suits for making false accusations. Expressions of concern made by school personnel about students' possible drug involvement or the act of reporting students who appear to be under the influence of drugs generally are not considered actionable as long as school personnel act in good faith and show reasonable cause by citing observed behaviors.

More often than not, however, the parents may be feeling alone, confused, and guilty. The call from the school, whether from a teacher, counselor, or principal, may be just what they needed to motivate them to seek professional help. Just as frequently, parents may not be aware of the extent of the problem or they may simply expect the school to solve it. Their active involvement in dealing with the problem, of course, is vital. If they are not notified, however, they cannot be brought into the process.

## Talking to Colleagues

Just as with parents, other teachers or school staff members also may have been concerned about the student but have said nothing until approached by someone with a similar concern. It is important, therefore, to consult with colleagues who have contact with the student. Once alerted by a concerned staff member, a counselor or assistant principal usually coordinates the comparing of notes on a particular student.

Some schools favor a more formal approach to identifying and dealing with student drug problems. They may designate a committee or team of professionals to receive all staff referrals of suspected drug abuse, and to conduct a preliminary assessment of a youngster's problem to determine if sufficient evidence exists for referral to a professional drug specialist for a formal assessment. This approach relieves individual teachers of the responsibility of confronting students and notifying parents. The "preassessment team" does it instead. The team often consists of a drug counselor, a teacher, the school nurse, and sometimes an administrator and student. Membership varies from place to place, but in most cases all members of the group receive special training, and at least one member receives advanced training in chemical substance abuse and preassessment techniques.

Because the behaviors associated with drug and alcohol abuse may also occur in connection with other problems, some schools use this centralized preassessment and referral process for dealing with any number of student problems, academic as well as behavioral, rather than focusing exclusively on drug abuse. Teachers and other staff are asked only to identify and document behaviors of concern. The preassessment team meets with the student, and often the parent as well, to determine if the problem can be dealt with at school or if referral for professional help is warranted. For example, a first-time offender caught in a school lavatory accepting a drag on a friend's marijuana cigarette may be issued a stiff punishment and given appropriate drug abuse information, while a longer-term user of drugs whose school and home situations have clearly deteriorated as a result of drugs would be referred to a professional assessment and rehabilitation program in the community. In general, then, the school needs to make an assessment that is adequate to make a sensible decision about the next most appropriate course of action.

Like the committees mandated by federal and state legislation on handicapped students, such teams may also recommend specific school program adaptations for students. It is not a good idea, however, to use the same committee that deals with special education for drug abuse and other behavioral problems unless the student is otherwise handicapped. Currently, drug dependency is not considered a handicapping condition under provisions of Public Law 94–142, the Education for All Handicapped Children Act, although recent attempts have been made in federal court to have this condition included in the federal law to guarantee such youngsters an individual education program specially designed to address their drug dependency.

In general, centralized preassessment and referral teams may be a useful way to organize a school's resources to respond to the problem of student abuse of alcohol and drugs. Great care should be taken, however, that such teams do not serve to encourage non-team members of the school staff to neglect or abandon their responsibilities to be vigilant and reach out to students in distress. The use of a school preassessment and referral team should not relieve teachers of the responsibility to take the steps outlined earlier in this chapter. It simply should make it easier for them to consult with and refer students to appropriate colleagues in the school.

## Referring and Helping the Student

Finally, teachers need to remember that they are not trained therapists or drug treatment professionals. The planning and implementation of an intervention program is the responsibility of the school's or the school system's pupil services team, or of the appropriate community agency or private practitioner. Teachers may be asked to provide information or help convince students to avail themselves of needed help. In less severe situations, a teacher or other staff member may be asked to participate in a support group for a student who needs help in coping with everyday problems. Such a group may be composed of a teacher, a counselor, and some "straight" friends of the student—each person being available to talk to or provide encouragement when necessary. Students who have stopped using drugs may also require such a support group to help them remain drug free. Helping young people discontinue the use of drugs can be extremely difficult, and each case is different. Therefore, referral to the counselor, the principal, the nurse, or designated others who can act as liaison with appropriate professionals is essential.

## Helping Versus Enforcing

A frequent source of frustration and confusion for school staff is the apparent conflict between the helping role and the enforcing role. Actually, both roles are appropriate and compatible. Students who are afraid to seek help from a teacher because they think the adult will "narc" on them should receive a careful explanation: if they seek help from the teacher, confidences (within limits) can be kept; but if they come to school in possession of drugs or under their influence, the teacher will not hesitate to report them.

What, then, should be the limits of the confidence that a teacher should maintain? Generally speaking, if a student comes to the teacher for help sincerely wanting to stop using drugs, the teacher should maintain confidences about past drug incidents so long as they do not continue to occur and the teacher is convinced that the youngster is making a good faith effort and agrees to get help. Individual school policy will determine specific discretion in this regard, however; teachers should check with their principals first to determine what confidences they are authorized to keep and under what circumstances. (See Appendix D for a sample policy on confidentiality.)

## Emergencies

Sometimes students who abuse drugs have severe psychological and physical reactions to the chemicals they put into their bodies. "Bad trips," or paranoia, panic, depression, hallucinations, and illusions, can lead to suicide or aggressive and bizarre behavior.[39] Long after the student has taken drugs such as PCP or LSD, a "flashback," or recurrence of the hallucinations and illusions, is possible. The real danger of a bad LSD trip is that the user, having lost touch with reality, will be injured by jumping out a window and expecting to float on air or by walking in traffic and expecting to be shielded from the impact of an oncoming truck.[40]

Severe negative effects of PCP include disorientation, anxiety, paranoia, hyperexcitability, hallucinations, feelings of impending doom and death, and violence.[41] Psychosis, a serious mental disorder characterized by personality disorganization, fragmented thoughts and feelings, and delusions and hallucinations, may develop within days of taking PCP. Here again, a danger exists that the user may be harmed because of a lack of good judgment. The anesthetic properties of the drug can cause the user to feel invulnerable to pain or serious injury, and to have delusions of great strength. At the same time, the PCP user may feel threatened by classmates and teachers who can appear as demons or monsters. In this state, the student may be dangerous to both self and others.

Cocaine, too, can cause a form of paranoid psychosis consisting of the hallucination that insects or snakes are crawling under or on the skin. The use of amphetamines also can produce this kind of hallucination as well as depression and delusions.[42] And long-term barbiturate use may result in paranoia and violence, as may the long-term use of alcohol or hashish, although not usually when used alone.[43]

The chances of a student experiencing such a violent reaction to drugs or alcohol while under a teacher's supervision are slight. Nevertheless, teachers should be prepared since it could happen. The following suggestions may help:

1. Stay calm; do not raise your voice, express anger, or in any way threaten the student.

2. Immediately notify the office to call for emergency help (police, paramedics, fire-rescue squad, or ambulance) and for help to physically restrain the student if needed.
3. Try to keep the class quiet, or if possible, remove the student to a quiet nonstimulating environment while waiting for professional help.[44]
4. Speak calmly and try to reassure the student that no one intends any harm.

Ask the student how much and what drugs have been taken. This information will be useful to the medical staff in determining how to treat the student. The primary concern should be to keep the youngster from doing harm to self and others, and to get professional help immediately. If the student reacts in a negative or frightened manner, stop talking and back off.

## The Role of the Principal

No discussion of the teacher's role in combating student drug abuse is useful without noting the tone-setting impact of the principal. Principals must not only understand and approve of the basic steps of the teacher intervention process, they must encourage and support faculty members as they implement them. This means that principals must take a leadership role by (1) providing opportunities at meetings and workshops for faculty to discuss drug use and rules, and teachers' roles in combating drug use; (2) publicizing to students, parents, and others that teachers are legitimately empowered to communicate their concerns to both students and parents; (3) providing professional personnel to whom teachers may refer students in need of counseling or other help; and (4) following up with students and/or parents when teachers feel they have fulfilled their responsibilities and can do no more.

## Other School Interventions

In addition to constructive and caring confrontation with students and parents, there are other interventions that schools have found effective. Group counseling sessions designed to screen for drug-related problems can be effective if well structured and run by a trained counselor. Some schools, however, have found that simply giving students opportunities to meet in small groups to "rap" is useful even if the adult leader is not a trained counselor. Such support groups can help students work through problems, find support from peers to stay "straight" and refuse drugs, cope with an alcoholic or abusive family situation, or stay off drugs after treatment. (See Chapters 6, 7, and 8 for additional information on support groups.) Other approaches have assigned kids to a form of in-school suspension where they spend one or more days each week in a drug education class learning about why they might be using drugs and how to stop.

Students who have received training as peer counselors and/or in drug abuse prevention can be effective in convincing their drug-abusing classmates to seek help. One strategy, for example, is to set up a drop-in center in a corner of the cafeteria, staffed by trained students. Posters and announcements publicize the availability of student volunteers to help kids with any problems or questions they might have: from concerns about a broken locker to getting help for a drug problem. The volunteers are given automatic access to a counselor and an assistant principal in case of need. During one such project conducted by a high school during the first 30 days of a new school year, a number of potential and current drug users referred themselves to other students who connected them with professional help. The drop-in center also functioned as a way of publicizing and enlisting volunteers for groups such as SADD (Students Against Driving Drunk) and other student-sponsored antidrug activities at the school.

# Training and Mobilizing

In most schools some staff members who are more interested in and committed to working on the drug problem than others can provide leadership in this area. Ideally, others can rally around or receive support and encouragement from these individuals. This "core group" should include at least one administrator and counselor in addition to teachers. Some groups include parents and students as well, depending upon how much experience the school has had working cooperatively with these constituencies. If possible, specialized training should be provided for this group, and subsequently more basic workshops for all staff. A number of groups around the country conduct such training. They will either come to the school, or staff or core groups can be sent to them for intensive training.

## School-Community Action Teams

One way of mobilizing to attack a school's drug and alcohol problem is to form a team of interested and committed persons representing teachers, students, administrators, counselors, other school employees, and the community-at-large (such as a member of the clergy, a police officer, or a rescue squad technician). The team representing a school-community coalition then undergoes intensive training, sometimes at a site away from the school, for about a week. Participants learn about drugs, their effects, why kids abuse them, and how to intervene and prevent student drug abuse. At the same time the team develops an action plan for dealing with the problem in their school and community.

In Maryland the state education department has made small grants available to individual high schools and their feeder middle school/junior high and elementary schools to help pay for consultants, materials, transportation, and other expenses associated with establishing these school-community action teams. Local school boards often supplement the team expenses, and community fundraising also helps pay part of the costs of implementing the action plan. Most plans involve a variety of prevention activities, some student early intervention such as peer counseling, and training activities for the rest of the staff and for groups at feeder schools.

## School Teams

Another training model with similarities to the school-community action team is the "School Team." Funds to implement this model come from matching grants by the Alcohol and Drug Abuse Education Program of the U.S. Department of Education. The goal of this approach is to help schools prevent and reduce drug abuse and associated destructive behaviors such as poor school performance, truancy, violence, vandalism, and dropping out. The grant is used (1) to help the school team develop a cooperative approach to school governance in which the entire school community assumes ownership of problems and takes part in their solutions, and (2) to help create and maintain a positive school climate to reduce destructive behaviors.

Residential training at a regional center is followed by back-home field training and technical assistance by consultants from the regional training center. As with the school-community action team, the school team—which consists of administrators, teachers, counselors, and a parent or other community member—also prepares an action plan for implementation. Student membership and involvement may come later as the school and team wish. The focus of this approach, however, is definitely on school staff.

The residential training includes the following:

1. A basic understanding of alcohol and drug abuse and related disruptive behaviors, their causes and

manifestations, and the current scene with respect to alcohol and drug abuse and related disruptive behaviors, and smoking

2. An understanding of young people and how they learn and develop their needs and expectations
3. Skills and experience in responsive educational approaches, such as communication, personal awareness, group process, and classroom management
4. A basic sensitivity to other cultures, lifestyles, social concepts, and mores
5. A basic understanding and overview of a variety of program strategies for prevention of substance abuse
6. Experience in interdisciplinary team building and working together as a cohesive unit
7. Skills in program planning and management, including needs assessment, identification of resources, techniques for developing a widespread support base, planning, management, and evaluation
8. A basic understanding of the school and school system as an organization, and of the management of organizational change.

In addition to implementing action plans that include training for colleagues and parents, counseling for kids, fundraising, and resource mobilization, school teams emphasize positive school governance and climate. They also focus on communication skill building, and problem-solving and conflict resolution workshops, as well as school policy revision. The involvement of school principals on the team promotes the sharing of decision making and greater consultation with staff around these and other issues.

As of this writing, over 4,000 school teams from small and large, urban, suburban, and rural schools throughout all regions of the nation have been trained through one of the five regional centers listed at the end of this chapter. On a more economical scale, staff from local drug treatment centers, hospitals, or health departments often are willing to conduct workshops for school staff free of charge. These workshops may focus on recognition, intervention, and referral. The opportunities for training are numerous. As with any new educational resource, however, previewing and screening a program before using it make good sense. This can be done by talking to people who have heard speakers or participated in training programs to find out if they will meet your particular needs.

## The School Survey

Before determining the school's action plan, either the administration or a concerned group should take stock of the school's strengths and weaknesses. Many schools have found that a simple, anonymous survey of students' attitudes toward and use of drugs is a helpful way to determine present conditions in the school. The survey may be expanded to include related areas of concern such as safety, race relations, and staff and student morale. An example of the type of questions asked: "I smoke marijuana more than once a week.—True or False." Or, "Most of my friends use drugs during school hours.—True or False." The state of Maryland conducts such a survey every two years and shares the results with local school officials. Information gathered from a school survey can also be supplemented by statistics from police and from school suspension or serious incident records.

From these data, areas of need can be identified rather easily. For example, if a significant percentage of students in a school indicates that they regularly smoke marijuana, or that they are aware of students stealing or extorting lunch money from others, that school has a problem. In any event, the school's action plan should be a response to an assessment, either formal or informal, of the school's needs. Generally speaking, teachers, students, and parents, as well as administrators, should have a voice in determining that plan.

## Working as a Team

The people, conditions, and factors influencing a youngster's drug abuse may be so intermeshed that altering one part of the picture without adjusting the others may prove ineffective. If the school decides to take action without involving the family, the primary influence on the student's life, its attempts probably will be fruitless. Alone, no one person or group can solve the problem. Each can take some steps to initiate the helping process, but everyone who affects the student's life must work together to develop a comprehensive response to deal with a youngster's drug problem. Within the school, teachers, administrators, counselors, coaches, all other employees, and students must cooperate. Schools in turn must involve parents as full partners.

In the community at large, individuals and groups already concerned and working on problems such as drunk driving, "head" shops, and law enforcement should be enlisted to help lobby government for appropriate treatment facilities and services for adolescents.

In a number of communities, existing social service or mental health agencies may be trying to deal with the problem on their own. They can no more do this alone than can the schools. Interagency cooperation also is a necessity. In Montgomery County, Maryland, for example, a joint project of the schools and the county health department, PACT II, uses drug counselors to work with students in need. These professionally trained therapists do an in-depth assessment of students referred to them by school personnel, parents, or the police and juvenile courts to determine (1) if they have a drug problem, (2) the severity of the problem, and (3) the appropriate kind of treatment needed. The PACT II counselors then assist the student, as well as the parents and siblings if they feel it is a family problem, to identify and receive treatment from particular hospitals, detoxification centers, therapists, or drug treatment centers as required. In certain instances, however, they may simply work with families, students, and school personnel to develop an in-school program or a combination of outside family therapy with in-school followup activities. At times these therapeutic counselors must counsel with the student, parents, and siblings to get them to the point where they realize they are in need of help and agree to accept treatment. In some cases, the school can help by refusing to readmit students unless they enter a treatment program.

A similar interagency approach is used by the Westchester (New York) County Department of Community Mental Health and local school systems with which it places Student Assistance Counselors. A description of this program is included in Chapter 6.

## Disciplinary Regulations and Policies

### Rules

Many persons believe that the best way to combat student drug abuse is for schools to establish and vigorously enforce strict rules regarding possession, use, and distribution of drugs. Fear of strict and immediate consequences, not concern for some future health impairment, they argue, will deter student drug use. Experience does show that any comprehensive plan to combat student drug and alcohol use in schools should include logically formulated rules with firmly and consistently enforced consequences. The more clearly and frequently communicated the rules, the more effective they will be.

A number of students, because they fear getting caught, may never begin to use drugs in the first place. Strict rules and close monitoring of bathrooms, stairwells, and school grounds, however, may result in driving many others elsewhere to use drugs. Weekend "partying" at unsupervised homes or shopping centers, as well as before and after school use of drugs, remains an inviting option for drug-abusing students.

Specific consequences will vary from school district to school district, depending upon state law, local sentiment, and the seriousness of the problem. Many schools impose mandatory three- to five-day suspensions for students caught under the influence and/or in possession of drugs. Since most drug possession is illegal, many schools also notify the police when they have proof of possession. Students caught distributing drugs and/or repeatedly using or possessing them may be expelled. In many schools, however, drug abuse rules are not consistently or regularly enforced.

## Enforcement

The zeal with which rules are enforced may be related to how recently the local news media publicized the problem or a tragedy such as a student death from overdose or drunk driving occurred in or near the community. To be effective, however, enforcement must be ongoing and consistent regardless of whether drug abuse happens to be a "hot issue" in the school or community at the time. Additionally, public schools must be careful to extend due process rights to all students and not to exclude them from school on suspicion alone. If a student claims illness and denies drug use, the school can usually do little in the absence of other proof. For this reason, it is most important not to rely solely on enforcement of disciplinary measures. A balanced approach is best. Students cannot always be forced into treatment as a condition for readmission to school, although it should be noted that most students who are heavily into drugs usually must be coerced in some way or other to enter treatment.

An important component of the enforcement effort in many high schools is the use of security assistants to monitor bathrooms, parking lots, stairwells, smoking areas, and halls. Although the use of such ancillary staff may help reduce the opportunity for students to use drugs on or around school premises, it does not, of course, solve the drug abuse problem.

School rules should make it easy for a student needing help to seek it without fear of reprisal. When a student seeks help from a teacher or counselor, disciplinary consequences need not be imposed. Discretionary privilege and maintenance of confidentiality may be reserved to school counselors. Teachers, nurses, and administrators also should be able to exercise these privileges, since students may not want or be able to seek out their counselor. In most instances, however, it makes more sense not to go beyond a promise of immunity from punishment for past offenses, and thus be free to share information with colleagues, parents, and treatment specialists.

## Policies

A good number of school systems have drug and alcohol abuse policies. Many of these policies, however, are general statements framed several years ago. A school system that does not have a policy should form a committee of teachers, administrators, counselors, parents, and representatives of the community agencies to frame one for the board of education's consideration. Likewise, any system whose policy was formulated more than five years ago should appoint a committee to review it. Well-thought-out, comprehensive school policies assure fair and consistent treatment and quality of service to students. They also clarify roles so that teachers will be certain about what actions they should undertake. (See Appendix D for an example of a state board of education policy on alcohol and other drugs.)

A good drug policy should include the following:

- The rationale or need for a school policy
- The relationship of drug use to other antisocial behaviors
- The commitment of the school to work with parents and the community at large to deal with the problem
- The commitment of the board of education to openly acknowledge any drug problem that may exist without any prejudicial effects on the school administration or staff
- Specific prevention and intervention procedures beginning in the elementary school
- Rules and consequences along with procedures for communicating these to students and parents
- Confidentiality, counseling, student peer involvement, and enforcement steps
- The assignment of specific roles to various job positions within the school
- The school's relationship with outside agencies such as police and social service departments.

## Take a Stand!

It does no good to be able to identify the problem if neither teacher nor school is ready and able to deal with it. When teachers have identified a student they feel may be abusing drugs, they should express concern and willingness to help the student and parent, and discuss it with the school nurse and/or the administrator designated to deal with this matter. Their goal should be to put a stop to the abuse for the protection of other students in the school and for the benefit of the abusing student, and to refer the student for help. Ignoring the problem will not solve anything and would be irresponsible.

In addition to the steps outlined earlier, teachers and all school employees can also help combat the drug problem in their school and community by standing up and being counted. For example:

1. Let people know that you do not approve of abusing drugs and alcohol. Let your students know in class discussions or in casual conversation that you unequivocally oppose the use of drugs and alcohol by youth. If you do not say anything, students and others may assume that you are not concerned or even that you approve of such practices. Whether you teach geography, health education, algebra, American literature, or fifth grade, sooner or later the opportunity will arise to let your students know exactly where you stand.
2. Be sure that your principal and other school administrators understand that you are concerned about childhood and adolescent substance abuse. If your school has a drug policy, let it be known that you expect it to be enforced. If your school does not have a drug policy, urge your colleagues to join you in calling for the development of one.
3. At budget time and at other times of the year, let your school board and other elected community leaders know that resources for drug education, prevention, and intervention, as well as staff training, should be made available.
4. If your school still provides student smoking areas, argue against them. Such areas send the wrong message to youth. They also put their health at risk. Students often use these areas to pass and use drugs.
5. Work with colleagues, parents, and others to establish a comprehensive plan to deal with drug use in your school, including
   a. Training of staff

b. Formulation of procedures for identification and referral of drug abusers
c. Establishment of both in-school and community early intervention and support programs
d. Access to community counseling and treatment resources
e. Implementation of awareness prevention, and education programs
f. Equitable and ongoing enforcement of rules and regulations.

In summary, while school personnel should not be expected to function as drug abuse counselors, nor should schools become treatment centers, both the school and the teacher have an important role to play in combating drug abuse. This and previous chapters have examined some identification, intervention, referral, and support functions appropriate to the school. Ensuring that students are referred to suitable assessment, counseling, and treatment services is a legitimate role for the school. The following chapter examines another important role for school involvement—prevention.

## Resources

### Assessing Drug Abuse Problems

Adolescent Assessment Project
919 Lafond Avenue
St. Paul, MN 55104
(612) 642–4029

This project has prepared an assessment model for determining the degree of drug dependence and designing clinical interventions for adolescents 12 to 20. It consists of a number of questionnaires and interview schedules for use by a trained chemical abuse professional. It may be useful to preassessment team members as well, or in training such staff.

McCarthy, Michael J. "A Model for the Chemical and Mental Health Assessment of Adolescents." Jamestown Adolescent Treatment Program, 11550 Jasmine Trail North, Stillwater, MN 55082. (612) 429-5307.

## Working with Minorities

Atkinson, D. R., and others. *Counseling American Minorities: A Cross-Cultural Perspective.* Dubuque, Iowa: William Brown Co., 1981.

Baron, A., Jr. *Explorations in Chicano Psychology.* New York: Praeger Publishing Co., 1981.

Page, J. B. "The Children of Exile: Relationships Between the Acculturation Process and Drug Use Among Cuban Youth." *Youth and Society* 11, no. 4 (1980): 431–47.

## Training Programs

"Reach America" Student Training Seminars
National Federation of Parents
1820 Franwall Avenue, Suite 16
Silver Spring, MD 20902
(301) 649–7100 or 800–544–KIDS

The School-Community Action Team Model has been used by a number of schools in Maryland. For information about the approach and for names and addresses of action team schools write or call

MADART Project Director
Maryland Department of Education
200 West Baltimore Street
Baltimore, MD 21201
(301) 659–2321

For specific descriptive and funding information about the School Team Approach, write or call the nearest regional training center or

Office of Alcohol and Drug Abuse Education
U.S. Department of Education
400 Maryland Avenue, SW, Room 2011
Mail Stop 6264, Building FOB-6
Washington, DC 20202
(202) 755–0410

*Northeast*

U.S. Department of Education
Alcohol and Drug Abuse Training
and Resource Center
Adelphi National Training Institute
P.O. Box 403
Sayville, NY 11782–0403
(516) 589–7022

*Southeast*

U.S. Department of Education
Alcohol and Drug Abuse Training
and Resource Center
5915 Ponce DeLeon Boulevard, Suite 11
Coral Gables, FL 33146
(305) 284–5741

*Southwest*

U.S. Department of Education
Alcohol and Drug Abuse Training
and Resource Center
Center for Educational Development
6800 Park Ten Boulevard, Suite 171 West
San Antonio, TX 78213
(512) 735–9191

*West*

U.S. Department of Education
Alcohol and Drug Abuse Training
and Resource Center
Region 8 Training and Development Center, Inc.
Box 9997 Mills College Station
Oakland, CA 94163
(415) 632–3775

*Midwest*
U.S. Department of Education
Alcohol and Drug Abuse Training
and Resource Center
2 North Riverside Plaza, Suite 821
Chicago, IL 60606–2653
(312) 726–2485

For information about other training materials and workshops contact

American Training Center, Inc.
P.O. Box 3140
Boulder, CO 80307
(303) 442–5010

Capabilities, Inc.
P.O. Box 318
Lexington, SC 29072

Community Intervention, Inc.
529 South 7th Street, Suite 570
Minneapolis, MN 55415
1–800–328–0417

Johnson Institute
10700 Olson Memorial Highway
Minneapolis, MN 55441
(612) 544–4165

PRIDE, Inc.
100 Edgewood Avenue, Suite 1216
Atlanta, GA 30303
800–241–7946
(24-hour hotline and tapes on drug and alcohol abuse)

## School Surveys

Tessler, Diane Jane. *Drugs, Kids, and Schools.* Glenview, Ill.: Scott, Foresman Co., 1980. pp. 113–29.

Crowley, James F. *Alliance for Change: A Plan for Community Action on Adolescent Drug Abuse.* Minneapolis: Community Intervention, 1984. Appendix B.

Nehemkis, Alexis, and others, eds. *Drug Abuse Instrument Handbook.* Rockville, Md.: National Institute of Mental Health, 1980.

This publication reproduces some 40 different surveys and provides descriptive summaries of each instrument. The book may be useful in choosing selected items.

Copies of the 113-question student survey administered to Maryland secondary school students every two years can be acquired by writing to

Chief of Management Information Services
Office of Management Information and Certification
Maryland Department of Health and Mental Hygiene
Drug Abuse Administration
201 West Preston Street
Baltimore, MD 21201
(301) 383–3959

The questionnaire surveys students' knowledge, attitudes, and experiences concerning the use of drugs and alcohol. Most schools would not want to use so many questions, but this instrument gives examples of good questions to ask.

A community drug and alcohol abuse survey will be supplied and processed for 25¢ per child or $50 for an unlimited number (as of 1986) by PRIDE, Inc. (100 Edgewood Avenue, Suite 1216, Atlanta, GA 30303).

## Teacher Intervention

Fornaciari, Suzanne. *How to Talk to Kids About Drugs.* Washington, D.C.: Potomac Press, 1980.

"A Better Place—A Better Time"
35-min. 16 mm color film available from
Community Intervention, Inc.
529 South 7th Street, Suite 570
Minneapolis, MN 55415

A good training guide, the film shows adults how to offer creative and varying levels of intervention for adolescent drug and alcohol use; it stresses the importance of rallying support for a team effort.

## Other Interventions

Muldoon, Joseph A., and Crowley, James F. *One Step Ahead: Early Intervention Strategies for Adolescent Drug Problems.* Minneapolis: Community Intervention, 1986.

The following are available from
Johnson Institute
510 First Avenue North
Minneapolis, MN 55403–1607
1–800–231–5165

*Intervention: A Professional Guide* (9 pp.)
This guide explains the steps involved in identifying the problem and training key persons for intervention.

*The Family Enablers* (16 pp.)
This booklet identifies and addresses the problem of how family members often make things worse by not dealing directly with their loved one's alcoholism. It has implications for all who refuse to deal directly with another's drug problem.

For specific information on group sessions integrated into the school day, contact the following:

*Insight Class:*

Community Intervention, Inc.
529 South 7th Street, Suite 570
Minneapolis, MN 55415
800–328–0417

*High School Awareness Center:*

Drug Abuse Coordinator
South Lakes High School
11400 South Lakes Drive
Reston, VA 22091

*Student Drop-In Center:*

Assistant Principal
Gaithersburg High School
Gaithersburg, MD 20877

*Students Helping Other Students (SHOP):*

Drug Abuse Prevention Coordinator
Howard County Public Schools
10910 Route 108
Ellicott City, MD 21043

## Working as a Team

Coordinator, Project PACT
Montgomery County Health Department
11141 Georgia Avenue, Suite 510
Wheaton, MD 20902

Crowley, James F. *Alliance for Change: A Plan for Community Action on Adolescent Drug Abuse.* Minneapolis: Community Intervention, 1984.

## Policies

*School Drug Policy: Overview and Recommendations.* NIDA. Washington, D.C.: Superintendent of Public Documents, U.S. Government Printing Office, 1986.

The National Institute on Drug Abuse (NIDA) (5600 Fishers Lane, Rockville, MD 20857) has copies of school system policies on drug and alcohol abuse and can recommend schools with good policies, as can the National School Boards Association (1680 Duke Street, Alexandria, VA 22314, [703] 838–6722), and the Public Affairs Staff, Drug Enforcement Administration (14th and I Streets, NW, Washington, DC 20537).

States that have recently developed comprehensive alcohol and drug policies include the following:

California State Department of Education
Health Education Office
721 Capital Mall
Sacramento, CA 95814
(916) 322–5420

Maryland State Department of Education
Division of Instruction
200 West Baltimore Street
Baltimore, MD 21201
(301) 659–2000

Minnesota State Department of Education
Drug Education Office
Capital Square Building, Room 658
550 Cedar Street
St. Paul, MN 55101
(612) 297–3913

New York State Department of Education
Bureau of Health and Drug Education
Room 960 EDA
Albany, NY 12234
(518) 474–1492

CHAPTER 6

# Preventing Student Drug Abuse

I think people look at drug abuse and think problems of this size are unmanageable. I don't buy that. This effort is worth it.

—Paul Newman

Just as there is no single cause of drug abuse, so too there is no single, or best, way to prevent it. Despite the absence of supporting evidence, however, many people long believed that simply providing information on the effects of drugs would deter children and adolescents from using them. In most cases, the information was factual, but during the 1960s it frequently contained "fear arousal messages" about the health and social consequences of using drugs. Unfortunately, most youngsters paid no attention to these scare tactics. During the 1970s, drug abuse prevention programs began to recognize and address the social and personality factors that contribute to drug abuse behaviors among children and adolescents. Through affective education, they attempted to eliminate the reasons students use drugs by meeting their emotional and social needs with social skills training programs.

## Principles of Prevention

Although many current drug and alcohol abuse prevention efforts are based on research results, as frequently happens, research presents mixed messages. Therefore, experience and old-fashioned common sense also must serve as guides. Some common sense principles follow.

## Use a Broad-Based Approach

To prevent drug abuse among students, a range of different strategies must be employed by school staff:

1. Deter drug use by limiting the availability of drugs on and around school property and imposing stiff and fairly enforced penalties for use, possession, and distribution.
2. Continue to provide information on the effects of drugs in a factual manner, emphasizing their short-term or immediate physical and social effects.
3. Provide social skills training, including how to cope with social pressures to use drugs, how to analyze the consequences of individual choices and identify alternative behaviors consistent with the individual's value system, and improving self-esteem.
4. Cooperate with the home and other agencies to provide more responsible and age-appropriate alternative activities that help youngsters increase their bonds with school, family, and community.

## Start Prevention Activities Earlier

According to some,[45] early age of drug use onset is the best predictor of serious abuse. Prevention efforts should begin before youngsters are faced with the decision, usually between 12 and 18 years of age. The need to begin in the elementary school is therefore critical. Special efforts should likewise be made to bolster prevention activities before especially traumatic and vulnerable times such as the transition to middle school/junior high and to senior high school.

## Help High-Risk Students First

We know from research, experience, and common sense that some kids are at greater risk of becoming drug abusers than others. Sometimes these children exhibit their vulnerability early in their school careers, but more often they are noticed in middle school/junior high and senior high school. This is not to say that prevention programs should not be offered to all students. When students are identified as being at high risk, they should be given additional help immediately. Some of the risk factors to look for include the following:

1. Poor parent-child relationship, including parental withdrawal of love, or abuse and neglect
2. Low self-esteem
3. Delinquency, disruptiveness, rebelliousness, or alienation
4. Low academic motivation
5. High degree of independence, and tolerance for risk-taking behavior
6. High degree of family and/or peer misuse of drugs
7. Early cigarette use
8. Psychological disturbance.[46]

Note that these factors appear to increase the probability of a youngster's subsequently abusing drugs. The signs, or symptoms, discussed in Chapter 4, on the other hand, may indicate that the youngster is already using them. This distinction is worth keeping in mind since the way teachers deal with a student who is already abusing drugs and one who has not yet begun to abuse them may be quite different. One factor that teachers may notice both before *and* after drug use is class cutting and truancy.

## Cover All Bases

Prevention efforts should be a continuum of interrelated and complementary activities including those at school, at home, and in the community. They should begin with preschool and extend through high school and beyond. They should extend beyond information and awareness to social-environmental, interpersonal, and behavioral factors. Since children become involved with drugs by starting with "gateway" substances like tobacco and alcohol, we must concentrate early in students' lives on showing them the dangers in using these harmful substances. Everyone's help should be enlisted, including that of successful non-drug-using students who can serve as positive peer role models.

## Schoolwide Activities

Activities that involve students before and after school, during lunch and free periods, and in assemblies still play an important role in most schools. Before examining what can be done to prevent student drug abuse in the classroom, let's look at some schoolwide activities.

Table 2, Grade Level Guide to Materials and Activities in Chapters 6, 7, and 8, will help teachers easily locate prevention materials and activities appropriate to the grade(s) they teach. The pictograms that appear in the margin next to each material or activity description will aid in quickly locating material for specific needs. (See page 102 for a key.)

### Homecoming Theme Corridors and Floats

Most high schools have a homecoming celebration each fall. Often sophomore, junior, and senior classes compete with one another in 9–12
decorating a corridor of the school building and/or in building a float for a parade or rally. Since this celebration usually accompanies a dance and a football game, opportunities for drinking and drug taking, why not encourage a "chemical-free fun" theme for the next homecoming activity? One of the classes—preferably the seniors so that they can act as examples to the juniors and sophomores—might

# TABLE 2
# GRADE LEVEL GUIDE TO MATERIALS AND ACTIVITIES IN CHAPTERS 6, 7, AND 8*

| Grade level | Materials and activities | |
|---|---|---|
| Grades K–3 | Here's Looking at You, Two 129<br>Alcohol and Other Drug Risk Reduction Project 131<br>Soozie and Katy 135<br>Project Charlie 130<br>Project DARE 133<br>Cross-Cultural Education 143 | CARE Center 165<br>Smoking Prevention 137<br>Strengthening Self-Concept 147<br>DUSO 150<br>Alliance Against Drugs 167<br>TESA 150<br>SAPE 166 |
| Grades 4–6 | Refusal Skills 136<br>Mass Media 139<br>Project Charlie 130<br>Book Reports 140<br>Marijuana, A Second Look 135<br>Student Compositions 140<br>Project DARE 133<br>Assemblies 103<br>Posters 142<br>Here's Looking at You, Two 129<br>Just Say No Club 107<br>Decision Making 138<br>CARE Center 165 | Alcohol and Other Drug Risk Reduction Project 131<br>Smoking Prevention 137<br>Strengthening Self-Concept 147<br>Magic Circle 150<br>Alliance Against Drugs 167<br>TESA 150<br>Natural Helpers Program 119<br>Mentor Program 106<br>SAPE 166<br>Student Publications 140 |

*Also see Resources at the end of each chapter for references to additional materials, activities, and programs that may not be described in the body of the text and are not reflected in this table.

| | | |
|---|---|---|
| Grades 7–9 | Refusal Skills 136<br>Mass Media 139<br>Student Publications 140<br>Project DARE 133<br>Book Reports 140<br>Drama 143<br>Student Compositions 140<br>Cross-Cultural Education 143<br>Posters 142<br>Saying No 107<br>ESL Social Skills 145<br>Assemblies 103<br>Materials for Black Youth 118<br>Just Say No Club 107<br>Ideas Booklet 145<br>Student Assistance Program 115<br>Alcohol Prevention 116<br>Mentor Program 106<br>Shock Trauma Unit Orientation 110 | CARE Center 165<br>Rescue Squad Orientation 110<br>Recovered Drug Abusers 111<br>You Asked For It 112<br>SADD 162<br>Support Groups 108<br>Peer Counseling 164<br>For Coaches Only 113<br>Natural Helpers 119<br>Strengthening Self-Concept 147<br>Here's Looking at You, Two 129<br>Alliance Against Drugs 167<br>Amazing Alternatives 132<br>Smoking Prevention 137<br>Decision Making 138<br>SAPE 166<br>TESA 150 |
| Grades 10–12 | Project DARE 133<br>Mass Media 139<br>Student Publications 140<br>Refusal Skills 136<br>Book Reports 140<br>Student Compositions 140<br>Cross-Cultural Education 143<br>Posters 142<br>ESL Social Skills 145<br>Drama 143<br>Materials for Black Youth 118<br>Homecoming Themes 99<br>Assemblies 103<br>Deterrents (Drunk Driving) 104<br>Alcohol Prevention 116<br>One-to-One Program 105<br>Support Groups 108<br>Student Assistance Program 115 | Mentor Program 106<br>You Asked For It 112<br>Shock Trauma Unit Orientation 110<br>Rescue Squad Orientation 110<br>Recovered Drug Abusers 111<br>For Coaches Only 113<br>SADD 162<br>Strengthening Self-Concept 147<br>Peer Counseling 164<br>Natural Helpers 119<br>CARE Centers 165<br>Here's Looking at You, Two 129<br>Alliance Against Drugs 167<br>Smoking Prevention 137<br>SAPE 166<br>TESA 150 |

# PICTOGRAMS

## Key to Use of Prevention Material/Activity

Grade Level for Material/Activity

Student-Implemented Activity

Minority-Specific Material

Parent-Implemented Activity

Interagency Community-Oriented Activity/Material

adopt a theme like "Having Fun Without Alcohol" and decorate their float or their school corridor with ideas for alternatives to getting high with chemicals, or "chemical-free highs"—for example, "Get High on Yourself" or "Get High on Life." Be sure to accentuate the positive, not spending time or placing emphasis on negative aspects that sound like lecturing or scolding. This idea also works for proms.

At the dance itself, music should be screened for pro-drug lyrics and, if possible, the playing of some antidrug records (or videos) should be encouraged. Because of adverse parent reaction in recent years to drug-oriented rock music, a number of entertainers now have begun to record songs and produce videos that are either free of such lyrics or openly antidrug. Stevie Wonder, Billy Joel, and Bob Seeger are examples of such artists.

## Assemblies

Plan to devote at least two assemblies each year to drug and alcohol abuse. Some of the more popular assemblies feature talks by sports, 4–12 music, or other celebrities whom students know and respect. The Reverend Jesse Jackson, for example, has visited a number of schools over the past several years to talk with students about drug and alcohol abuse. Frequently professional athletes, rock stars, or TV personalities are happy to make themselves available to speak with kids, if only they are asked. The recent scandals in professional athletics make positive role models from among those ranks more important than ever.

Be sure to find out the content of the talk as well as the speaker's approach before the presentation begins. A staff member can meet or speak on the telephone with the visitor in advance to provide guidelines. Also, plan followup activities such as compositions in English or discussions in social studies. In addition, student involvement in inviting and introducing the speaker gives the activity an air of acceptability. If possible, try not to have the entire school or a full auditorium present. The most effective assemblies are those with audience-speaker interaction; this is better accomplished when only one group, such as the sophomore or junior class, attends at one time. Always follow up the speaker with information on where to find help. Invariably, some students who are abusing drugs will be moved to want to get help. While they are willing and motivated, counselors or others who can refer them to treatment should be available to talk to them.

Another assembly idea especially effective at prom time is called "Scared Stiff." This presentation usually involves a police officer or traffic safety professional (sometimes from a state highway agency or an automobile club) who tries to impress upon sophomores, juniors, and seniors the deadly game they play when drinking and driving. It includes slides of automobile accidents and case histories of tragedies that have occurred in the town or city, and, in some cases, that have involved students at the high school. While some have eschewed the scared stiff approach as unnecessarily negative, others have found it realistic and its effects on kids sobering and effective. The important thing to remember in such a presentation is not to exaggerate to create an effect. In the case of drinking and driving, there is no need to do so.

Other large group presentations can entertain at the same time they deliver a message about drugs and alcohol. Students in elementary school grades, particularly, are impressed by jugglers, musicians, mimes, storytellers, and others whose performance is used as a culminating activity of a health education or science unit on drugs and alcohol. One such performer, a former high school drama teacher, specializes in teaching fourth through sixth graders "to juggle and not take drugs," by entertaining them while he explodes drug myths and discusses alternatives. Drug education that engages young students' attention and delivers the message "how to say no when someone in middle school next year offers you drugs" can be accomplished in such assemblies or large group activities (two or three individual classes in a building). Many packaged programs of this type are available commercially.

## Drunk Driving Deterrents

9–12

At prom time police departments in some communities will tow to a school wrecks of cars demolished by teenagers in accidents involving drinking. The wrecks are displayed on the school's front lawn or other conspicuous location. Details of the accident—names and ages of people killed—are displayed by the wreck along with admonitions such as "Friends don't let friends drive drunk," or "If you drink, don't drive; if you drive, don't drink."

One high school devotes part of a corridor wall to this information. The names and dates of death, as well as a quote from the student driving the car that killed his friends, are painted on the wall in bold letters for all to see and think about during the entire school year.

Another very successful program to deter drinking and driving among high school students is Project Graduation, a campaign to promote alcohol-free activities and prevent alcohol and drug-related accidents during the high school prom and graduation season. In many communities the campaign is promoted through radio, TV, and newspaper ads; posters and buttons; and printed reminders in tuxedo pockets, corsage boxes, and delivered with caps and gowns. These printed themes, such as the Washington, D.C., area's "Arrive Alive—Don't drink and drive," may also appear on restaurant tables or hang from police and fire station windows. In addition, free taxi rides home from the prom or graduation parties for those who feel they are in no condition to drive or who do not want to ride with one who has been drinking are also provided with no questions asked.

Most Project Graduation campaigns are sponsored by schools, parent groups, student groups, local businesses, and police or other government agencies, all working together for a safe prom and graduation season. Packets consisting of wallet cards with emergency information, bumper stickers, buttons, posters, and a host of pamphlets on the dangers of drinking and driving are often made available to parents and students in the weeks before the prom season.

Finally, some schools find it effective to show films like *The Last Prom*, a poignant story of teenage tragedy caused by driving drunk at this time of year.

## One-to-One-Program

A prevention approach tried at Southfield Senior High School in Michigan makes high school faculty or adults available on a one-to- 9–12 one basis to talk with kids. Teenagers with tight schedules often have no one to talk to in a large high school. It may be impossible for them to find an adult who is available when they are. The One-to-One program was instituted for students and adults to get together just to talk, either about general topics or about particular problems if necessary. The idea, formulated by counselor Susan Pearce and math teacher Iva Gould, grew from the realization that one of the keys to student success is establishing a personal relationship with an adult—one who will take a particular interest in the student, one who the student feels will really care.

The program includes not only teachers and counselors but janitors, food service workers, secretaries—any persons who work at the school because they like kids and want to help. Ms. Gould receives one hour of released time each day to match students (who self-refer or are recommended for the One-to-One) with one of the 45 adults (out of 110) who have signed up. Each staff/student pair meets at least once a week, either at lunch or before or after school. School officials report that students turn to the program for many reasons such as trying to improve attendance or grades, needing a friend to help until they become comfortable in their new environment, or needing an adult role model that may be lacking at home. The program is careful not to usurp the role of the parent or guidance counselor but tries to supplement these roles. Talking with an adult staff member first often makes students feel more comfortable discussing concerns with their parents. Occasionally a staff volunteer identifies a serious problem and refers the more seriously troubled students to counselors for professional help.

## Mentor Model

The Mentor Model also has been
used by several schools in districts all over the
country to address the problem of drug abuse as it
4–12 affects students' attitudes, behavior, and school

achievement. Although the model is designed to help students gain as much as possible from their school experience, it has applications to mastery of personal goals as well. Students meet regularly with a mentor or adviser to build communication, organization, study, and leadership skills.

In some schools the mentor may hold small group meetings or plan activities for two to four assigned students. Schools have adopted and adapted the model in many ways, but the common thread of all these programs is the significant relationship that exists between mentor and student. The student comes to respect the mentor as a person and professional, as one who has values, hopes, wisdom, and strengths that the student hopes to acquire. The mentor cares for, teaches, challenges, and supports the student.

The Mentor Model can be an effective vehicle for providing support to students who are experiencing difficulties with drug or alcohol abuse, and it can be an effective prevention program by supplying students with the coping strategies needed to avoid drug involvement.

## Just Say No Clubs

A NIDA-sponsored activity that is sometimes useful with children, particularly those in
junior high, intermediate, and middle schools, is the 4–9
"Just Say No" Club. This program offers booklets, pins, buttons, and tee shirts emblazoned with the slogan "Just Say No." In effect, it helps students say no when their peers pressure them to smoke, to take dope, to drink. It gives them a reason and a way to say no that saves face and that bolsters their self-esteem. The materials are attractive, simple, and straightforward, and seem to be effective, particularly with younger children. The first Just Say No groups were started in Oakland, California, with the eight-year-old star of ABC's "Punky Brewster Show," Soleil Moon Frye, doing a weekly half-hour

community service program. Soleil is now the national chairperson of all Just Say No groups, which are proliferating in schools and communities across the country, particularly in elementary and middle and junior high schools.

Even when children have not tried drugs or alcohol themselves, most know others who have and are deeply affected. The concept of Just Say No groups is based on several key ideas:

- Changing the acceptance of the youth drug culture; getting young people to see drug use as a serious potential health hazard
- Getting young people to make a strong public commitment to remain drug free
- Involving kids against drugs at an early age.

Anyone can organize a Just Say No group: a high school student, several students working together, teachers, counselors, parents, law enforcement personnel, members of the clergy, other interested community members. Most clubs comfortably handle 15 to 20 members each, hold regular meetings, and emphasize giving all members a chance to participate and lead. The aim is to change the prodrug peer culture. Information, advice, and ideas on how to start these groups, what activities have been successful elsewhere, how frequently to hold meetings, and how to network with other groups are available from NIDA.

## Support Groups

Some young people find it is not easy to stay straight when it seems that everyone around them takes drugs. For these students, many high
7–12 schools provide support or "rap" groups. Such groups offer the opportunity to meet and be positively reinforced by like-minded peers, or to express concerns and get help with problems. Other kinds of groups common in some schools are those for kids

who (1) live with an alcoholic or drug-abusing family member, (2) use drugs but are trying to stop, and (3) have been through some type of formal alcohol or drug treatment and need support to keep from backsliding. In most cases, each type of group meets separately, but occasionally a group made up of predominantly one type of student—say, "abstainers"—may include a student in a different category, such as one who uses drugs but wants to stop.

Students are referred to support groups by counselors, administrators, teachers, or themselves; but typically a counselor interviews and approves students for a group. Eligibility criteria for an abstinence support group may include such factors as the following:

1. A desire to stay drug free
2. An ability to benefit from the group process
3. A need to ease pressure on a student.

The organization and professional staff involvement of support groups may vary but most groups generally follow these ground rules:

1. After the initial session, students make a commitment to attend a specified number of sessions.
2. Groups meet weekly, usually during lunch or an activity period; or the period when they meet is rotated each week so that the same class is not missed repeatedly.
3. Confidentiality is maintained in the group.
4. An adult staff member acts as the group leader, with peer counselors functioning as co-leaders.
5. Groups do not try to provide therapy.
6. Group members always address their comments to each other and the group; there are no side conversations.
7. Groups should remain small enough for everyone to participate fully—say, no larger than seven or eight students.

## Visiting Shock-Trauma Units

7–12

One school sends its eleventh graders through an orientation to the shock-trauma unit of a nearby hospital. The program has three stages. First, staff from the hospital and a health education teacher or assistant principal working with a few classes at a time describe and discuss the purpose, workings, and eligible patients of the unit, with emphasis on drug overdose cases and victims of auto accidents that involved alcohol or drugs. The next day, or within a week, students visit the hospital and meet and talk with physicians, technicians, and nurses before and after they visit the unit and observe emergency cases in treatment. Finally, students engage in followup activities at school either by completing individual assignments or by doing a group project such as a school display, a spot announcement, or a presentation for other students.

## Rescue Squad Orientation

7–12

Another school uses the local fire department rescue squad team to get across the message that drugs are serious business. At a group meeting to discuss drugs, a student simulates a psychotic PCP episode or jumps up from the audience, yelling, "Oh, my God, I'm flying," and seems to pass out on the floor. The activity is staged beforehand for dramatic effect unknown to the student audience. Then another person yells, "Call the rescue squad." As if by magic, the squad arrives within several minutes and goes through the motions of emergency treatment. The whole subterfuge lasts only about six or seven minutes before students are told that the victim is OK and that the incident is a simulation to demonstrate what happens when kids take certain drugs. During the staged incident, adults watch the student audience carefully to see if anyone reacts with undue stress or alarm. The remaining presentation describes what the rescue squad technicians do in such cases and possible effects of the drug in question.

## Recovered and Recovering Drug Abusers

6–12

A number of years ago a popular approach among some drug prevention specialists was to invite recovered drug abusers to speak to "straight" students about their experiences. This approach fell into disfavor mainly because the reformed abusers often had an unintended opposite effect on their listeners. Youngsters looked at these seemingly healthy and respected recovered abusers in a romanticized way. Additionally, some recovered abusers openly admitted to their young audiences that they still used drugs from time to time.

Careful screening of recovered drug abusers is therefore extremely important, as is the case with anyone who is to address students on this topic. Inviting youngsters who are currently in drug treatment programs to speak at faculty meetings can be a productive activity for both teachers and youngsters. It is a good idea, however, not to invite students from the same school in order to avoid inhibiting both faculty and student speakers from sharing perceptions of each other's behavior relating to the problem of student drug abuse. Teachers who have listened to and interacted candidly with students in treatment and their therapists or drug counselors have rated these activities among the most interesting and professionally rewarding of any they have attended.

At such meetings the kids share how and why they started using drugs, what drugs they abused and how often, and if and how they used drugs before or during school hours. Teachers are usually particularly interested in students' perceptions of what their teachers thought about their drug use and whether they believed that the teachers were aware of it. In addition, most faculty find it valuable to hear students share their feelings about whether their teachers cared about them and what they could have done to help.

Recovered drug abusers can also be

effective in talking to peers about the effects of drug use on their lives. Such presenters should be screened first to determine that (1) they do not currently use drugs or intend to use them; (2) their attitudes toward drug use by peers are appropriate to the purpose of a prevention activity; and (3) they are articulate, willing to participate, and likely to profit from the experience themselves. Done well, with sincerity and intelligence, presentations by recovered abusers can be a positive influence in dissuading peers from experimenting. Done in a haphazard or unplanned manner, these activities can do more harm than good.

## You Asked For It

7–12

Among the many commercial and public agency-prepared booklets prepared for teenagers on the subject of drugs is one entitled *You Asked For It: Information on Alcohol, Other Drugs and Teenagers.* This well-prepared, easy-to-read, 24-page booklet covers just about everything that should be covered on the subject without overwhelming or turning off the student:

- What is a drug?
- Some words to know
- Using drugs and abusing drugs
- Drug facts
- Drugs, sex, and reproduction
- Drugs' effects on driving, school, and sports
- Dealing with peer pressure
- Handling drug problems
- Talking with your parents about drugs
- Feeling good without drugs.

This publication, available from the Wisconsin Clearinghouse, is perfect for mass distribution to students or as a handout to at-risk students.

# For Coaches Only

6–12

Schoolwide prevention activities can start with a particular cross-section of students. With the high visibility and peer respect given athletes, school efforts targeted for this population can be effective. The Department of Justice Drug Enforcement Administration publishes a packet of materials aimed at high school coaches. One booklet, *For Coaches Only: How to Start a Drug Prevention Program,* is a challenge to coaches to take advantage of their special relationship with young people. They are in contact with many of the opinion makers and status leaders of the school and have a tremendous impact on them. It encourages coaches to make sure that their athletes are not using, abusing, or condoning the use of drugs or alcohol. It suggests that they make a survey to see exactly what the problem is, if one exists, among athletes in their school. Recent studies have shown that alcohol and drug use among student athletes may be very serious in certain schools. The booklet asks coaches first to find out how much they know about their players, to become aware of their problems, situations, and habits.

The second challenge is for coaches to do something about preventing the drug problem on their teams. In particular they are told that they can—

- Make themselves knowledgeable, just like everyone else, about the symptoms of drug abuse and be able to recognize the signs.
- Call their captains together and talk about drug abuse.
- Open a dialogue with athletes on alcohol and drug abuse.
- Persuade the athletes in their school to use pressure on teammates to refrain from the use of drugs and alcohol.
- Enforce training rules and school regulations, sometimes better than others can.

- Advise athletes of the legal penalties of drug use.
- Develop a plan for dealing with drug abuse.
- Set up conferences with parents.
- Check on their athletes—call them at home, let them know that they are watching and they care.
- Investigate violations and confront athletes immediately.
- Take immediate action when they overhear party plans that might involve drugs and alcohol being talked about in the locker room.
- Confront their players immediately when they smell alcohol or detect some other drug.
- Do something about snuff, which is known to be a cause of cancer and which is popular among some athletes.
- Try to counteract the negative publicity about alcohol and drug abuse problems among professional athletes that permeates the media.
- Try to counteract the beer and snuff commercials that give kids the impression that good athletes use these drugs.
- Finally, set a good example for the students.

The Drug Enforcement Administration also publishes a booklet called *Team Up for Drug Prevention*, a set of specific action plans that coaches can adopt. This packet of information includes the following printed material:

1. The effects of drugs on young people
2. Reasons why athletes use alcohol and other drugs
3. Enabling behaviors for coaches (things coaches may or may not do that unwittingly support student drug use)
4. Responsibilities of coaches regarding chemical abuse
5. Suggestions to coaches on starting a drug prevention program for athletes

6. Nine steps for drug prevention programs for athletes
7. Suggestions for captains when dealing with their teammates
8. Sample survey to give to athletes on their drug use
9. Sample letter to parents
10. Sample survey of coaches.

The activities enumerated in this packet are practical and simple, they require no money and little extra time, and they are appropriate to the coach's overall job description and responsibility.

## Student Assistance Program

Based on the employee assistance program model found in industry and in some larger school systems throughout the United States, the 7-12
student assistance program uses professional counselors to provide primary prevention and early intervention services. One successful interagency version of this approach, which has been adopted by a number of communities around the nation, is the Westchester County Student Assistance Program. In this model counselors are accountable to both the community mental health agency that employs them and the school where they are based.

Students may be referred to the program counselors by school staff who are concerned about a student problem, or by the parents or students themselves. Those found under the influence of drugs or alcohol on school grounds or at school activities are required to enter the program. Counseling groups are a major source of assistance to students, striving to help them improve self-esteem and their ability to cope with school and family problems. Preventive support groups for newcomers and seniors who will soon leave school for work or college also are conducted to help strengthen their defenses during these periods of vulnerability. Students not ready for group involvement are counseled individually. Counselors also conduct family sessions for those needing and requesting help and make referrals to community treatment agencies and private practitioners when necessary. In addition, they make presentations at faculty meetings and provide consultations on individual students and student activities.

## Alcohol Prevention

7–12

Alcohol is perhaps the most devastating of all drugs for young people, accounting for ruined lives, death, and tragedy in great proportion. The National Institute on Alcohol Abuse and Alcoholism publishes a great many materials on adolescent alcohol abuse prevention. One such publication, *On the Sidelines: An Adult Leader Guide for Youth Alcohol Programs,* contains ideas, suggestions, and alcohol education concepts from youth leaders across the country. Its purpose is to help adults stimulate and support alcohol abuse prevention projects "carried out by youth, for youth, on issues that interest and affect them."[47] A companion booklet, *Is Beer a Four-Letter Word?*, gives 12 project ideas for preventing alcohol abuse among adolescents. It starts with a look at one's roots, and family and community influences and attitudes toward drinking. Other action plans include the following:

- Working with a local disc jockey to get messages across to kids who are listeners
- Suggesting alternatives to drinking that can be promoted
- Setting up student support centers
- Arranging drinking and driving demonstrations that can be carried out in driver education classes
- Staging experiments with peer pressure
- Opening drop-in centers or so-called dry discos
- Producing creative assembly programs.

The booklet lists numerous sources of information, including pamphlets, booklets, films, and other resources that can be used with a variety of groups; the costs of specific materials; and the names, addresses, and telephone numbers of people who have successfully implemented these programs. It also provides suggestions and information on how to begin working with youngsters. Finally, it lists sources of help in the 50 states and the territories of the United States.

## Minority Group-Oriented Activities

Schools can respond to the problem of drug and alcohol abuse among minority youth by—

K–12

1. Bolstering feelings of self-worth and pride in students' ethnic groups and/or race
2. Introducing positive role models into school activities at assemblies and through books, films, and other media
3. Using bilingual and other minority staff and volunteers in schools to provide support and understanding, and to facilitate home-school communication
4. Training school staff in cross-cultural sensitivity and understanding
5. Offering a variety of cultural activities in which both students and parents can participate during the school year
6. Offering instructional and language accommodations to newly arrived, limited-English-speaking students
7. Developing cooperative relationships between schools and native language and/or minority-oriented helping agencies in the community, and holding workshops for parents to acquaint them with these services
8. Teaching and practicing problem-solving, decision-making, goal-setting, and social defense skills

9. Supporting recreational and other alternative activities to drug use.

## Programs and Materials for Black Youth

Although not nearly enough attention is being paid to minority-oriented programs and materials, some government agencies and national
7–12 health organizations do publish non-English-language versions and specially prepared editions of drug and alcohol abuse-related materials. Commercial publishers also are beginning to produce more minority-oriented materials. Minority interest groups likewise are a good source of information about such materials and programs.

In response to urging by a panel of Black experts constituted by the National Institute on Alcohol Abuse and Alcoholism, the Institute prepared a *Guidebook for Planning Alcohol Prevention Programs for Black Youth*. In Black and other minority communities, treatment of alcohol and drug problems traditionally has taken precedence over prevention activities. According to the *Guidebook*, "Black Americans represent the largest ethnic minority group in the United States, yet alcohol programming for this group has been limited and is often not sensitive to cultural differences and values." Chapters in the *Guidebook* cover the following topics:

- Black history, with an emphasis on alcohol use among Black Americans, and the experience of Black youth with drinking
- Prevention approaches and reasons why traditional programs for white youngsters have often been unsuccessful with Black youth
- Nine alcohol prevention strategies suitable for use with Blacks
- How to start prevention programs by involving the community
- Resources with information on operating Black

youth programs, as well as names and addresses of national, state, and local organizations.

Examples of activities and materials especially designed for use with non-English-speaking and American Indian students also are included in Chapter 7.

## Natural Helpers Program

This program is a peer and adult counseling approach designed to help adolescents within a school deal with problems such as mood 5–12
changes, and difficulties with friends, families, schools, and drugs. The premise behind the Natural Helpers Program is that students with problems naturally seek out other students and occasionally teachers or other school staff whom they trust. They ask them for advice, for help in getting assistance, or just to provide a sympathetic ear. Using this existing network, the Natural Helpers Program provides training to students and adults who are already serving as informal helpers in the school. It gives them the skills they need to more effectively help young people who seek them out.

People in a school who are natural helpers can probably be readily identified. Certain students, teachers, administrators, counselors, or other staff members because of their position or their personality—as a coach, or as a student leader, or as a friendly kid who is popular or very approachable—are all candidates. The Natural Helpers Program uses existing peer networks wherever possible. It identifies the helpers by means of a survey, thus assuring that students and staff selected are already viewed as trustworthy. It provides specific kinds of training in communication skills, decision making, problem solving, referral, and other helping activities. The program tries to identify the typical problems faced by students and to provide the helpers with information relevant to those problems. It also establishes situations where helpers can use their skills to help others and it tries to support the helpers in dealing with their own problems as well as those they encounter in helping others.

Other features of the program include better student use of professional help available in the school and in the community, focusing on specific issues of concern whether they happen to be drugs or sex or safety issues, and reducing feelings of alienation by providing easy access to helpers who share similar values.

## Resources

### Prevention Research

*Prevention Research* (NIDA Research Monograph 63) is available from the National Clearinghouse for Drug Abuse Information, P.O. Box 416, Kensington, MD 20795 ([301] 443–6500).

*Essentials of Adolescence* Quarterly Newsletter is available from People Science, 168 Woodbridge Avenue, Highland Park, NJ 08904.

### Schoolwide Activities

Rock songs, records, and videos that have antidrug lyrics include the following:

*Don't Drive Drunk*, Stevie Wonder
Motown Records (1985)

*Stop the Madness*, Tim Reed
Tim Reed Productions (1986)

*You're Only Human*, Billy Joel (antisuicide)
Columbia Records

*Johnny, Come Home*, Fine Young Canibals (antirunaway)
IRS Records

*White Lines*, Grandmaster Melle Mel
Sugar Hill Records

*King Heroin*, Jazzy Jeff (rappin')
Zombia/Artista Records

*Smuggler's Blues*, Glen Frey (Miami Vice)
MCA Records

*Ashes to Ashes*, David Bowie
RCA Records

*Like a Rock*, Bob Seeger and the Silver Bullet Band
Capitol Records (1986)

Assemblies—Tim Moss/Creative Hand, Box 3311, Arlington, VA 22203 ([703] 528-3408), provides "drug education that works" for grades 4 to 8 for a fee in the Washington, D.C., area. State drug abuse prevention agencies (see Appendix A) probably can suggest the names of persons in other areas who offer similar services.

For information on how a California-based organization enlists professional athletes to act as positive role models and to help combat substance abuse, write

Pros for Kids
1519 South B Street
San Mateo, CA 94402
(415) 571-0726

A useful anti-drunk-driving film is

*The Last Prom* (23 min.)
Southerby Productions, Inc.
5000 E. Anaheim Street
Long Beach, CA 90804
(213) 498-6088

Another excellent awareness film for adolescents, featuring the music of Huey Lewis and the News, is

*Too Good to Waste* (22 min.)
FMS Productions, Inc.
P.O. Box 4428, 520 East Montecito Street
Santa Barbara, CA 93140
800-421-4609 or (805) 564-2488

Reader's Digest has identified 115 student-developed programs for combating drinking and driving through a $500,000 college scholarship contest. For a list and more information write

Reader's Digest Public Relations
Pleasantville, NY 10570
(914) 241–5385

Project Graduation information can be obtained from most national parent groups, NIDA, or NIAA, or from

Washington Regional Alcohol Program
1705 DeSales Street, NW, Suite 300
Washington, DC 20036
(202) 293–2273

One-to-One Program—For information on how the One-to-One Program works at Southfield Senior High School write to

Ms. Susan Pearce
Southfield Senior High School
Southfield, MI 48034

Mentor Model—For one school district's experiences with the Mentor Model, contact

Director of Quality Integrated Education
Montgomery County Public Schools
850 Hungerford Drive
Rockville, MD 20850

"Just Say No" Clubs—Pamphlets for kids, booklets for organizers, and "Just Say No" flyers on drugs and their effects are available in English or Spanish from NIDA.

"Just Say No" tee shirts, bumper stickers, and pins are available from

Parents in Action
c/o Pacific Institute
7101 Wisconsin Avenue, Suite 612
Bethesda, MD 20814

Support Groups—For guidelines and advice on setting up support groups contact

Children Are People, Inc. (K–6)
493 Selby Avenue
St. Paul, MN 55102
(612) 227–4031

Community Intervention
529 South 7th Street, Suite 570
Minneapolis, MN 55415
1–800–328–0417

New Beginnings
1325 Everett Court
Lakewood, CO 80215
(303) 231–9090

Shock-Trauma Unit—
Assistant Principal (CODAA)
Bethesda-Chevy Chase High School
4301 East-West Highway
Bethesda, MD 20814

Rescue Squad—
Assistant Principal
Gaithersburg High School
314 South Frederick Avenue
Gaithersburg, MD 20877

*You Asked For It: Information on Alcohol, Other Drugs, and Teenagers*, as well as a number of other publications and posters on youth and drugs, is available from

Wisconsin Clearinghouse
1954 East Washington Avenue
Madison, WI 53704–5291
(608) 263–2797

*For Coaches Only* and its companion booklet *Team Up for Drug Prevention* are available from

U.S. Department of Justice
Drug Enforcement Administration
Washington, DC 20537

*On the Sidelines* and *Is Beer a Four-Letter Word?* may be obtained from

National Clearinghouse for Alcohol Information
P.O. Box 2345
Rockville, MD 20852

For information on the student assistance program, write

Director, Student Assistance Program
Westchester County Department of Community Mental Health
112 East Plains Road (2d Floor)
White Plains, NY 10601
(914) 285–5260

*Preventing Alcohol Problems Through a Student Assistance Program, A Manual for Implementation Based on the Westchester County, New York, Model.* National Institute on Alcohol Abuse and Alcoholism. Washington, D.C.: Superintendent of Documents, U.S. Government Printing Office, 1984.

## Minority Group-Oriented Activities

Harrison-Burns, Bettye, and others. *A Guide to Multicultural Drug Abuse Prevention: Strategies Series Booklet*. NIDA. Washington, D.C.: Superintendent of Documents, U.S. Government Printing Office, 1981.

See also *Resources Series Booklet* and *Needs Assessment Series Booklet* in the above NIDA series.

*A Guidebook for Planning Alcohol Prevention Programs for Black Youth* is available from

National Institute on Alcohol Abuse and Alcoholism
U.S. Department of Health and Human Services
Alcohol, Drug Abuse, and Mental Health
5600 Fishers Lane
Rockville, MD 20857

For information on race-specific training/workshops, consultation, and resources including books, radio and TV public service announcements, and posters contact

Minnesota Institute on Black Chemical Abuse
2616 Nicollet Avenue South
Minneapolis, MN 55408

For a description of a Refugee Parent Training Program dealing with student drug abuse prevention, contact

Bilingual Office
c/o Central Middle School
Main Street
Murphreesboro, TN 37130
(615) 890–5728

Two references useful in working with Southeast Asian refugee students and their families are

Owan, Tom Choken, and others, eds. *Southeast Asian Mental Health: Treatment, Prevention, Services, Training and Research*. Rockville, Md.: National Institute of Mental Health, Division of Prevention and Special Mental Health Programs, 5600 Fishers Lane, 1985.

*A Guide for Helping Refugees Adjust to Their New Life in the United States*. Washington, D.C.: Center for Applied Linguistics, 3520 Prospect St., N.W., 1981.

The following are some suggested background readings in the area of minority student drug and alcohol abuse and risk factors:

Au Nguyen, Thuy-Phuong. "Positive Self-Concept in the Vietnamese Bilingual Child." *Bilingual Journal* 8 (Spring 1984): 9–14.

Banks, James A. "Black Youths in Predominantly White Suburbs: An Exploratory Study of Their Attitudes and Self-Concept." *Journal of Negro Education* 53 (Winter 1984): 3–17.

Ford, Denyce S. "Self-Concept and Perception of School Atmosphere Among Urban Junior High School Students." *Journal of Negro Education* 54 (Winter 1985): 82–88.

Grossman, Fred, and Retish, Paul M. "Classroom Counseling: An Approach to Improve Student Self-Concept." *Counseling and Values* 21 (October 1976): 64–66.

Humm-Delgado, Denise, and Delgado, Melvin. "Hispanic Adolescents and Substance Abuse: Issues for the 1980's." *Child and Youth Services* 6 (Spring-Summer 1983): 71–87.

Morgan, Monica C., and others. "Subcultural Differences in Alcohol Use Among Youth." *Journal of Adolescent Health Care* 5 (July 1984): 191–95.

Moreno, Steve. *Vamos a Hablar del Abuso de las Drogas (Let's Talk About Drug Abuse)*, 1981. Available from Moreno Educational Co., 6837 Elaine Way, San Diego, CA 92120 [(714) 461–0565].

Other booklets in this Spanish-English Series:

*Padres Aprenden Acerca de las Drogas (Parents Learn About Drugs)*

*Como Usar la Disciplina Preventiva y la Recompensa Positiva con Sus Hijos (Preventive Discipline and Positive Rewards)*

*Los Efectos de la Tension en los Padres y la Vida Familiar (The Effects of Stress on Parents and Family Life)*

*Padres: Aprenden Sobre Sus Hijos Adolescentes (Parents: Learn About Your Teenagers)*

*Padres: Estas Son Algunas Ideas para Poder Comunicarse con Sus Hijos Adolescentes (Parents: Some Ideas for Communicating with Your Teenagers)*

Tam Thi, Dang Wei. *Vietnamese Refugee Students, A Handbook for School Personnel*. 2d ed. Springfield, Ill.: MOMD, 1980. Available from National Dissemination Center, 417 Rock St., Fall River, MA 02720

Videocassette:

*My Last Chance in Life,*
*Maury Wills Talks About Drugs*
Color (12 min.)
Lawren Productions, Inc.
P.O. Box 666
Mendocino, CA 95460

The following is available from National Clearinghouse for Bilingual Education, 1555 Wilson Boulevard, Suite 605, Rosslyn, VA 22209, 800-336-4560:

Saville-Troike, Muriel. *A Guide to Culture in the Classroom*, 1978.

## Natural Helpers

A *Natural Helpers Program* manual is available from

Comprehensive Health Education Foundation
20832 Pacific Highway South
Seattle, WA 98188
(206) 824-2907

# Prevention Materials and Activities for the Classroom

I'm not really into drugs, but wherever I am there's lots of cocaine and marijuana use. I feel really uncomfortable at these parties when it's all around me.

—Shawn, age 15

## Health and Drug Abuse Curricula

Historically, drug abuse prevention programs were built on the assumption that children and adolescents used drugs because they were ignorant of the consequences of using them. Such ignorance, it was reasoned, resulted in neutral or even favorable attitudes toward experimentation and/or regular use. Now we understand that drug abuse is associated with a variety of social, intrapersonal, and behavioral factors as well.[48] Most health education curricula today are therefore a great deal more comprehensive. Sample curricula and materials are available from state education departments, local school systems, public and private agencies like NIDA or the American Lung Association, and commercial educational text and materials publishers. Most of them build on the research that emphasizes self-esteem, decision making, refusal skills, and pertinent information about the effects of drugs. And almost all begin at an earlier age. Some of these curricula are highlighted in the following pages.

## Here's Looking at You, Two

K-12

The National Institute on Alcohol Abuse and Alcoholism (NIAAA) prepared a K–12 drug and alcohol curriculum called "Here's Looking at You, Two," in Seattle, Washington, in 1979. This curriculum provides a self-contained set of sequential activities at each grade level designed to achieve a cumulative effect. It includes a teacher training component and has been field-tested in a number of communities and states. NIAAA received positive feedback through its evaluation of the curriculum. The program provides specific drug and alcohol information, high-quality creative materials that are easy to use, and a mechanism for continued evaluation and revision of these materials that permits the incorporation of up-to-date information. The program's philosophy is that the incidence of alcohol and drug abuse among young people will decrease if they have a greater degree of self-esteem, are better able to cope with life's problems, have current facts about alcohol and other drugs, and are more skilled in handling interpersonal relationships.

The basic objectives of the program include the following:

1. *Information*—to expose youth to the basic facts about the physiological, psychological, and sociological implications of drug and alcohol use, and to teach them how to gather information about alcohol and drugs; to distinguish between reliable and unreliable, and relevant and irrelevant information.
2. *Analysis*—to help youngsters identify and define problems; gather information; brainstorm alternatives; predict consequences associated with different choices and behaviors; identify analysis factors such as attitudes, values, feelings, emotions, pressures from peers and families, risk levels and habits; develop action plans on the basis of these analyses and evaluate the appropriateness of their actions.

3. *Coping skills*—to help students gain skills in identifying sources of stress in their lives, to recognize when they are stressed and its effects on them; to identify mechanisms for coping with the stress and determining consequences of the coping behaviors.
4. *Self-concept*—to help young people increase their self-awareness by helping them identify what is important to them in their lives; to help them recognize their feelings and know how to express them by explaining how they feel about themselves and identifying their various roles and activities, as well as increasing positive self-concepts so that students can identify their own personal strengths and weaknesses and develop skills in selecting and practicing changed behaviors.

Each objective or area of objectives is repeated in each grade level throughout the curriculum. For example, information on drugs and alcohol starts in kindergarten and first grade when students learn why substances cannot be identified just by looking at, tasting, or smelling them. Elementary and middle school/junior high students make an in-depth study of controlled substances, and senior high students receive alcohol and drug information from research, speakers, and films. Other areas such as problem solving, coping skills, and self-concept are also dealt with at each grade level.

## Project Charlie

K–6

This K–6 curriculum has over 35 lessons designed for classroom use once a week. It focuses on the following:

- Self-awareness and self-esteem
- Relationships
- Decision-making skills
- Chemical use (taught only in grades 4 through 6).

Project Charlie (Chemical Abuse Resolution Lies in Education) staff teach the lessons in the Edina, Minnesota, schools where the private, nonprofit organization that developed the program is based. Since its inception nine years ago, the project has trained 3,500 teachers in 23 states and 4 Canadian provinces. The curriculum is based on research findings about what drug-abusing youngsters have in common: the need for building social competence and positive self-concept. Project Charlie's assumption is that before drug information can be helpful to them, children need to have social competencies: a positive self-image, the confidence and skills to say no, and the ability to deal with stress. Charlie also aims at building a partnership between school and family to teach children crucial living skills. It teaches kids to respect and feel good about themselves and others, and to make healthy decisions; and it encourages parents to become involved and continue discussions at home. In the classroom Project Charlie emphasizes communications, particularly the skill of listening, in an environment that is open, trusting, and supportive.

## Alcohol/Other Drug Risk Reduction Project

K–6

This project is a kindergarten through grade 6 health curriculum developed by the Washington Area Council on Alcoholism and Drug Abuse (WACADA) with inner-city minority children under a grant from the U.S. Center for Disease Control in Atlanta. It was field-tested from 1980 to 1984 in Washington, D.C. The curriculum content guide includes a program designed to be integrated into the core curriculum of each grade. Infused into art projects, songs, games, science experiments, language arts, history, and math, these learning experiences give students a well-balanced program of substance abuse education as well as effective ways of coping with the world today.

This curriculum is unique in that it is particularly useful for inner-city children where drug and alcohol abuse may be common occurrences for elementary school-age youngsters. It assumes that children already know a great deal about alcohol, tobacco, and other drugs, and have been exposed to them either in their homes or neighborhoods, or in the community at large. The content focuses on identification of alcohol, tobacco, and other drug products; physical effects of alcohol and other drugs; environmental effects; environmental influences dealing with the family, society, and peers; and the defenses against substance abuse such as risk taking, decision making, coping skills, and self-awareness. This curriculum is currently in use in many Washington, D.C., public elementary schools.

## Amazing Alternatives

7–9

One program being field-tested in eight junior high schools in Minnesota teaches kids to recognize and practice alternatives to using drugs, in addition to many other approaches to preventing drug use. The program, known as Amazing Alternatives, consists of discussions of the following topics led by elected and trained peer leaders:

1. The immediate and long-term consequences of drug use
2. Why kids take drugs
3. Analysis of the factors that influence kids to take drugs
4. Finding alternatives to drug use that meet these same needs
5. Developing counterarguments to drug-inducing media influences
6. Identifying and resisting peer pressure
7. Learning how to be an assertive nondrug user
8. Making a public commitment to continue not to use drugs.

Some of the schools include additional components beyond the classroom sessions:

1. Newsletters to parents on parent-child communication about drugs
2. Explanations of school rules on drugs by peer leaders (on videotape)
3. An "Alternatives Week" planned by peer leaders, promoting and reinforcing health-enhancing alternative activities and behaviors
4. Assistance to parents who desire to stop smoking.

## Project DARE

5–12

A successful interagency effort to help elementary and middle school/junior high school students resist peer pressure to experiment with drugs is the Drug Abuse Resistance Education (DARE) project of the Los Angeles Police Department and the Los Angeles Unified School District. Here, too, the goal is to teach kids to say no, not after but before experimenting and as peer pressure begins.

The DARE curriculum consists of 17 lessons taught by Los Angeles police officers on full-time duty with the project. Each officer is assigned five schools each semester (usually fifth and sixth grades) to visit on a weekly basis to present a curriculum prepared by school health specialists. These carefully selected line officers, all with many years of street experience, are fully trained by school district personnel who carefully monitor their classroom performance. In addition to the elementary school program, a middle school/junior high school curriculum, coupled with early intervention counseling of high-risk students by school counselors, is also being implemented.

The DARE curriculum consists of the following 17 classroom sessions conducted by the police officer, followed up by activities taught by the classroom teacher:

1. Practices for personal safety

2. Drug use and misuse
3. Consequences of using or choosing not to use drugs
4. Resisting pressure to use drugs
5. Resistance techniques: ways to say no
6. Building self-esteem
7. Assertiveness: how to exercise your rights without interfering with others' rights
8. Managing stress without taking drugs
9. Media influences on drug use
10. Decision making and risk taking
11. Alternatives to drug abuse
12. Alternative activities
13. An officer-planned lesson for a particular class
14. Role modeling: a visit by a high school student who is a positive role model
15. Summarizing and assessing learning
16. Composing essays or writing letters on how to respond to pressure to use drugs
17. Schoolwide assembly to award DARE students their certificates of achievement.

## Curriculum and Other Program Materials

Curriculum materials and instructional media useful for drug and alcohol prevention are more plentiful today than ever before. In addition to the various commercial materials, a number of short courses and/or materials are available from government agencies and public service groups, many of them free of charge.

## Elementary School Prevention Program Coloring Book

K–3

As part of the President's drug awareness campaign, the U.S. Drug Enforcement Administration publishes a coloring book called *Soozie and Katy*, featuring a kangaroo, Soozie, and a frog, Katy. The book, containing 21 different illustrations that children can color, is aimed at students in kindergarten through third grade. Its purpose is to counteract the advertising that bombards children and to help them learn that drugs are not a cure-all for problems—that they are meant to be taken only for illness. A teacher's study guide at the beginning of the coloring book explains how to use each of the 21 illustrations to get across a particular point. The illustrations lead to discussions about feelings and staying healthy, the role of doctors and pharmacists in the delivery of drugs in the health system, the symbols for prescriptions, and the effects of drugs on the body. The last two illustrations are designed to determine whether the children have digested all the information; and at the end of the program each child receives a certificate signed by Soozie and Katy.

## Marijuana, A Second Look

3–6

Organizations such as the American Lung Association, in cooperation with the American Council for Drug Education and the Weekly Reader, have published some fine curriculum materials. One publication, *Marijuana, A Second Look*, comes with a teacher's guide and features characters from the television show "Fame." Because of the wide use of marijuana among young people, this health education program aims at children ages 9, 10, and 11. It tries to help them explode some of the myths about marijuana, explain why it is harmful, and learn how to say no when pressured to use it now or in the future. The program uses a "Fame Fantastics" magazine, a Fame poster with a drug message, a fitness followup, and a play activity.

## Refusal Skills

Because of the research findings supporting the effectiveness of this approach in preventing the onset of cigarette smoking among students, a
3-11 number of commercial refusal skills materials are beginning to appear. Two examples are the *Saying No to Alcohol and Drugs* film (or video) and the Refusal Skills teacher training and support materials.

The film is designed for children 9 through 12—ages at which students may have heard about but not yet experimented with alcohol or drugs. It presents ways to say no to peers, under various types of pressure, when offered drugs. It also tries to build self-confidence and assertiveness, and to establish awareness of positive alternatives to drug use among its viewers. Finally, it explores reasons why young people get involved with alcohol and drugs, and their effect on health and performance. Valerie Brisco-Hooks, winner of three gold medals at the 1984 Olympics at Los Angeles, hosts the presentation.

The Refusal Skills program aims at helping students resist peer pressure by means of specific behavioral steps. Trained staff members model the steps for students who are then required to perform them in front of a videotape recorder and camera. After viewing their performance and receiving feedback, students practice the skills until they achieve mastery. The Refusal Skills teaching module supports the "Here's Looking at You, Two" drug and alcohol curriculum.

The program offers teacher training workshops, a videotape, and computer software that allows students to learn/reinforce the skills using the Apple IIE computer, as well as followup and practice activities that can be conducted after students have completed work on the computer. The Refusal Skills program has been used most often in schools in Washington and a few other western states. While considered especially helpful in upper elementary and junior high school grades, it has been implemented in third grade through high school classrooms with students of all ability levels.

## Smoking Prevention

The American Cancer Society publishes a packet of materials on smoking prevention available free of charge. It includes an envelope 3–12
containing two buttons: one illustrated with a frog wearing lipstick, saying, "Kiss Me, I Don't Smoke"; the other with flowers, saying, "Smoking Stinks." A booklet for elementary school-age youngsters entitled *Huff and Puff* tells how the story of the big bad wolf and the three little pigs got turned around because the wolf smoked and was unable to huff and puff and blow anything down. Consequently when asked, "Who's afraid of the big bad wolf?" the answer is, "Nobody, if he smokes." The packet also contains pamphlets on the dangers of smoking, how to stop smoking, some myths about stopping smoking, the dangers of chewing tobacco or snuff, facts on lung cancer, and "15 Most Often Asked Questions About Smoking and Health and Their Answers." Other materials in the packet include a comic book featuring some multiracial Marvel comic characters and a coloring book for elementary youngsters entitled *The Story of a Cigarette.*

For older students, the American Cancer Society distributes "Smoking Prevention," a packet containing a multicolored, 8½ × 11-inch scientific booklet, *The Beleaguered Lung, Cancer Invades*, with overlays of physiological depictions of the lungs and the various tissues affected by lung cancer. This publication is suitable for a high school or middle school/junior high biology class. A newspaper-like sheet called "The Cigarette Paper" with the headline "Teen Smoking Trends—What's New," features a report on the increased smoking of girls ages 12 to 18 over that of boys, some tips to help quit smoking, and other articles of interest. Finally the packet contains a sheet of cutout "Kiss Me, I Don't Smoke" decals that can be mounted to make extra copies of the button. The American Cancer Society will send this material free of charge upon request. Local chapters are listed in local telephone directories.

## Decision Making

5–9

*This Side Up* is a popular NIDA booklet for intermediate, junior high, and perhaps first-year high school students. Subtitled *Making Decisions About Drugs*, it has been used extensively around the country. Although scheduled for revision soon, the booklet still serves as a very useful source of information for young people faced with making decisions about drugs. The 64-page publication features cartoons, multicolored layouts, and an easy-to-understand and -read format. It begins with a description of various drugs and their effects. It continues with a down-to-earth discussion of why some people take drugs, and then examines the "fine art of the fast answer," which is another approach to how to say no to pressures to take drugs. The next topic, "Taking Risks," deals with decision making, self-esteem, risking rejection, and seeking acceptance from peers.

A section called "Getting to Know Me" deals again with making choices and thinking about the self and the individual's value system. The publication ends with tips for alternatives to getting high called "mind trips." Several mind trips are suggested for kids to take alone or with others. Some suggestions are very helpful and appeal to youngsters; others are somewhat infantile and may not be well received by adolescents. In general, however, the book is useful for drug education or health classes, or for a good discussion piece for an extracurricular group or a group counseling session.

# In-Class Activities

The teacher's impact on student attitudes, knowledge, and opinions is greatest in the classroom. The classroom, therefore, should be a major focus of prevention activities in the school. Regardless of subject or grade level, most if not all teachers can do *something* to infuse drug and alcohol prevention into their subject and/or class space. The following pages describe activities that can be implemented in connection with the regular curriculum and that do not require the teacher to be an expert on the subject.

## Mass Media

5–12

Film, drama, and journalism students can write and produce their own videotape on drug/alcohol abuse prevention. Providing information, resources, and technical process skills and advice will help students produce a well-thought-out, quality product that has the added appeal of approaching adolescents from their peers' point of view. Schools with TV studios and daily student-authored news bulletins also can air student-produced drug prevention messages. Discuss the role of television as the preeminent mass medium among children and adolescents, and the effect the alcohol and drug modeling behavior they observe on TV and in other media may have. Discuss the fact that alcohol is the most frequently advertised beverage in television programming, and that its use is generally depicted as promoting positive consequences.[49]

Discuss the fact that most mass media drug prevention campaigns have failed to change behavior because they have not reached the intended audience and have relied on information and fear messages.[50] Have students analyze some TV or radio public service announcements similar to those done by the Lung Association or the U.S. Department of Health and Human Services, and see if they can do better on their closed circuit productions, videotapes, or the public address system.

## Student Publications

In a program sponsored by the Washington Area Council on Alcohol and Drug Abuse (WACADA), students 13–18 reviewed literature on
5–12 drug and alcohol abuse and wrote their own pamphlet directed at their peers. The result, *Rappin' About Drugs*, was so well received that the 50,000 published copies ran out in six months. Other classes might also research, write, and publish a drug prevention booklet.

## Book Reports

Be sure the school library/media center contains books and other materials at all interest and reading levels on drug and alcohol abuse, espe-
4–12 cially inspirational stories of children, adolescents, adults, and, in particular, celebrities or sports figures who have overcome these problems. Encourage youngsters to read some of the books for reports and research projects.

## Student Compositions

In February 1985, the National Institute on Drug Abuse (NIDA) published *Teens in Action: Creating a Drug-Free Future for America's
6–11 Youth*. The book describes the experiences of 15 teenagers who either became involved with drugs and later stopped or who successfully resisted the pressure to use drugs. All the teens describe their experiences in starting prevention programs in their own homes, schools, and communities. Adolescents can easily identify with these young people and many

find their stories inspirational. The book can be used in English, social studies, health, or science classes. Teachers can ask students to read the book and then write about their personal observations, attitudes, and actions regarding drug and alcohol prevention.

Recently NIDA tried out the book with students at Takoma Park Junior High School (Maryland), a school with a culturally, ethnically, and socioeconomically diverse student body. In conjunction with the school's English department, NIDA held an orientation for about 600 students, briefing them about the project. The students viewed six public service announcements related to drugs and alcohol, and two music videos whose theme was resisting drug and alcohol use. NIDA also invited two of the original fifteen teen authors to talk to the students about the pressures they faced to use drugs and alcohol and how they successfully resisted them. English teachers gave all students assignments to write about at least one or two of the items listed as "Profiles for Action"—"Who am I?" "Several things that are important to me right now," "Why I think young people use drugs and alcohol," "How much I care about others," and "Are drugs and alcohol a problem for young people in my school, community, or for me?"

Students wrote essays of about 500 words—some very personal and specific, others more general and removed. Each student did a first, intermediate, and final draft of the assignment within a two-week period. Teachers selected the best profile for each class and winners received prizes donated by a local service club as awards. NIDA and Takoma Park Junior High also agreed to publish a booklet that included the profiles written by the prize-winning students with their pictures and names on the cover. A local TV station paid for the printing. At the end of the project NIDA sought feedback from English teachers at Takoma Park Junior High. All of them thought it was a valuable experience that fit well into the English curriculum and said they would recommend it to others. The teachers felt that the assignment helped students not only to learn about drug and alcohol issues, but also to take stock of their own attitudes, and to improve their writing and communication skills.

Other schools can try a similar project. It is low cost and easy to replicate, and can reach many students. It can also generate a number of school spinoff activities, such as discussions or debates with the "celebrity kids," and a pool of student speakers who can visit other schools such as feeder elementaries to discuss the topic.

## Posters

4–12

A number of agencies and commercial concerns produce some very creative and appealing posters that are well received by adolescents. A poster in the classroom (with the name, address, and telephone number of a community drug counseling service or a crisis hotline added in a corner or at the bottom) can serve many purposes: (a) as a conversation piece and an excuse to let people know where the teacher stands on the issue of drug and alcohol abuse, (b) as a positive reminder to students in the classroom of the message against abusing drugs and alcohol, and (c) as a source of information on where to get help that might be used by someone in the class who would otherwise be hesitant about asking an educator for such information.

Some of the national suppliers of posters, as well as various drug education curriculum companies, are listed at the end of this chapter. Many of these groups send their materials free of charge. Although most of the posters are aimed at older adolescents, some may be useful for intermediate, middle, and junior high school students. Teachers who cannot find any may have their students create their own posters, and see if a local public relations or printing company will print them in quantity for the school.

## Drama

9–12

Speech and drama classes sometimes can use plays or dramatic presentations with drug and alcohol themes to satisfy their curriculum needs. One such play, *Booze*, is available from the Addiction Research Foundation. It runs about 60 minutes and consists of six separate vignettes that can be performed as individual pieces or presented in sequence in one performance. With a few exceptions, all the characters play middle-class high school students. Students who have put on the skits enjoy the programs; they also become more critical of alcohol abuse and more supportive of social control.

Some teens write and perform their own drug abuse skits, portraying themes of peer pressure, the effects of taking drugs, and the results of drug dependence. These works are then performed for peers and students in middle school/junior high and elementary school with followup discussions with the audience. Often the student performers profit even more than their student audience. If well planned, however, both groups can benefit from this activity.

## Cross-Cultural Education

7–12

Although not yet plentiful, some cultural awareness materials are available for use with students new to the United States. In addition to books and films about other cultures, specific instructional materials and teaching techniques may be employed to help both refugee and native-born students become more aware and understanding of their own and others' cultures. In her book on *Cultural Awareness Teaching Techniques*, Jan Gaston gives teachers (particularly those who teach English as a second language) suggestions for helping students in a multicultural classroom better understand the new culture without the stress and feelings of inadequacy that refugees often experience and that may help contribute to drug use. Gaston arranges the twenty techniques in the book into four stages of cultural awareness:

1. Beginning the process by introducing students to the concept that culture pervades our lives and different cultures are organized in different ways

2. Reacting to cultural differences by giving students the opportunity to practice the skill of coping with ambiguity in a constructive way

3. Accepting selected aspects of the target culture by participating in it as fully as feasible while at the same time students surrender some of their own culturally bound ways of behaving

4. Learning more about the target culture and building attitudes of respect for both their own and others' cultures by helping students develop skills and attitudes that are useful for interacting with other cultures.

Gaston offers exercises that help students realize that what we observe is affected by past experiences (culture, family, and interests) and that generalizations can be dangerous and unfair (for example, "All Americans are rich"). In particular, she attempts to get students to examine the stereotypes they and others hold, to understand how and why they were formed, and to realize that often they are invalid and lead to misunderstandings.

To combat the stress produced by racial stereotyping, a number of books and films for various age groups are available from the Council on
2–9 Interracial Books for Children. In one, *The Secret of Goodasme*, space creatures discuss stereotypes with a white girl, a Black boy, and a Cherokee boy, convincing the children that (1) stereotypes are not true, (2) stereotypes cause harm, and (3) stereotypes are used to justify unfair treatment of women and minorities.

## Teaching Social Skills in the ESL Classroom

Many teachers of English as a second language (ESL) use materials that help their students develop such social skills as making decisions, get- 7–12
ting along with others, coping with authority, and identifying and accepting their own feelings while they learn to speak, read, and write English. Barbara Bowers and John Godfrey's Canadian text *Decisions*, for example, uses a problem-solving format to develop English language skills. Each of its 16 chapters presents students with relevant open-ended problems and offers a number of possible solutions, leading to analysis, discussion, and role-playing activities commensurate with students' linguistic abilities.

For teachers wishing to help students with making choices, getting along with friends, and coping with authority, Janus Books publishes a series of language development books that present multicultural teens in realistic, interesting situations. Two other books, for intermediate to advanced level English as a second language students, focus on helping youngsters understand and express their feelings. *Acceptance to Zeal: Functional Dialogues for Students of English* tries to help students express and understand a range of desires, needs, feelings, emotions, convictions, and attitudes through dialogue and role play. Students who cannot express their feelings in English are at risk for stress and frustration. *Feelings* by Doff and Jones likewise teaches students to talk about, understand, and express their own and others' feelings in a variety of social situations.

## Ideas Booklet

A source of ideas for seventh and eighth grade classroom teachers is a 1981 NIDA publication entitled *Saying No, Drug Abuse Prevention/Ideas for the Classroom*. The activities in this 7–8
booklet include such curriculum areas as art, physi-

cal education, health, social studies, language arts, science, and math. Two of the activities, one in math and one in physical education, follow.

Math—Rank Ordering Options for Decisions

Time Required: One to two days

Objective: To develop students' awareness of rank-ordering techniques, to encourage increased computational skills.

Method: Explain the concept and use of rank-ordering techniques to your students. On paper, describe five decision-making situations relevant to your students and the pressures they face. Outline four to seven options for behavior in each situation. Examples might be:

A. What would you do if one day your best friend refused to talk with you?
   ____ refuse to talk to him/her?
   ____ ask him/her what was wrong?
   ____ talk to a friend who knows you both?
   ____ talk to your parents?
   ____ get mad and start an argument with your friend?

B. What would you do if all your friends started to smoke and kept pushing you to do the same?
   ____ try one and stop there?
   ____ start smoking?
   ____ say no but still hang around with them?
   ____ stay away from them?
   ____ talk to your parents about the situation?
   ____ tell them you snort coke instead?

Method: Give each of your students a copy of the situations, asking them to individually rank order the options, according to what they would do in each case. Form small groups (five or six per group) and provide time for students to discuss their rank orders, sharing the reasons for their choices. Ask each group to determine a group rank order. Bring the class together as one group, so that each small group may report its group rank order to the class. Compare the small group rank orders, and if time permits, develop a total class rank order. Ask students to share their reactions to the situations and the task of making decisions about the options.

Physical Education—The Impact of "Put-Downs" on Participation

Time Required: One to three days

Objective: To increase student awareness of "put-downs" on students' participation in sports activities.

Method: After at least two weeks of team sports activities, ask students to individually write down one put-down they have heard sometime during the team sports activities. Explain to the students that these put-downs will be read out loud to the rest of the class. Collect the put-downs, and one at a time, let students draw one from the pile, read it to the class, and describe how they would feel if someone had made such a statement to them. Time permitting, role play PE situations in which put-downs are likely to occur; role play ways in which the situations could be handled without the use of a put-down. Ask students to think of ways in which put-downs pressure a person—especially in a team sports setting. Explain the concept of self-image to students, perhaps by telling the IALAC (I Am Lovable And Capable—Sid Simon) or Claude Steiner's Warm Fuzzy Story. Ask students to draw a relationship between the strength of a person's self-image and his/her willingness to participate in sports activities. Ask students to individually write down positive statements that would encourage rather than discourage them from playing with others in the class. Collect these statements; without comment, read them out loud to the class. Save the positive statements. When appropriate or necessary, suggest that students choose a positive statement rather than a put-down as a way of communicating to someone else in the class.

These activities are examples from which others can be spun off. They are based on the strategy of helping kids understand the pressures from peers that are so strong at this time in their lives and also learn how to resist these pressures when they run counter to their values and good judgment.

## Strengthening Self-Concept and Developing Social Skills

Because low self-esteem and inadequate personal and interpersonal skills increase the likelihood of drug use, building positive self-concept in students has been regarded as an effective way to prevent drug and alcohol abuse. To date, however, research on the effectiveness of this approach has been mixed.[51] Studies of prevention approaches using training in such social skills as communicating, problem solving, decision making, and recognizing and resisting pressures to use drugs have tended to show more positive results.[52] Among the newer self-esteem and social skills curricula that have shown positive results in decreasing alcohol abuse is the "Here's Looking at You" program, especially when begun before middle school/junior high.[53] Low self-concept is associated with failure and with behaviors that lead youngsters to negative actions; therefore educators continue to be concerned with enhancing their students' self-image. Youngsters who have a low self-concept often believe that failure is caused by low ability, and they usually have a low opinion of their ability. Often, they may—

- Give up easily.
- Procrastinate.
- Deny that they can do things, and do not even want to try.
- Have difficulty making decisions.
- Set unrealistically high or low goals for themselves.
- Punish themselves when they fail.
- Exhibit anxiety about school work.
- Exhibit low expectations for their own performance.[54]

School factors that contribute to low self-concept are said to include the following:

- Too much competition in the classroom, grouping and comparing students with one another
- Competitive evaluation and testing that is overdone
- Emphasizing ability rather than effort
- Communicating low expectations to students
- Expressing sympathy toward these students
- Allowing students to be uninvolved in classroom learning
- Using punitive discipline practices.[55]

K–12

Strategies for enhancing self-concept and motivation may include the following:

1. Reduce competition (praising low self-concept children does not help to raise their self-concept—the way they think needs changing) by (a) using cooperative learning techniques, (b) individualizing instruction, (c) communicating performance expectations in advance, and (d) avoiding social comparisons.
2. Promote beliefs in their own competence by (a) giving individual feedback to students and helping them make plans for improvement, (b) designing tasks that are neither too easy nor too hard, (c) making success available to more students, and (d) communicating positive expectations.
3. Promote trial-and-error approaches by (a) letting students keep track of the number of trials until they achieve success, (b) modeling this approach in selected lessons, (c) focusing on effort expended as opposed to success or failure, (d) showing interest in student progress, and (e) emphasizing effort expended in games and tasks.
4. Encourage realistic goal setting by (a) making grades contingent upon meeting one's goals, and (b) practicing goal setting.
5. Increase involvement in learning by (a) using flexible scheduling and self-pacing, (b) relating the curriculum to the students' experiences, and (c) making sure each student has something to contribute.
6. Increase chances for success by (a) training children in friendship-making skills, (b) providing intensive academic skill training, and (c) using peer tutors.
7. Reduce anxiety (time constraints on tests often add to anxiety and affect the results of the test) by (a) using a variety of grading practices, (b) communicating expected behaviors in advance, and (c) creating a positive, supportive climate.

8. Provide for affective needs by (a) using activities that encourage self-reinforcement, and (b) using procedures that encourage peer support.[56]

The basics of building positive self-concepts are the same for an elementary or a secondary school class: having positive expectations; praising students for their attempts; stressing effort, not giving students work they cannot do; making sure each student's strength is set off to advantage so that he or she can demonstrate it at some time; listening to and respecting students so they will listen to and respect the teacher.

Self-esteem building techniques also include recognizing and accepting feelings such as joy, anger, fear, disappointment, or affection. Two
K–3 self-esteem building programs that are available and
4–6 have proved useful are DUSO and Magic Circle (the human development program). DUSO (Developing Understanding of Self and Others) is a kit designed for the primary grades that relies heavily on storytelling, puppets, audiotapes, and songs. Magic Circle is more appropriate for the upper elementary grades; it requires more concentration and more focused listening skills than DUSO since the main activity involves children talking and listening to each other.

## TESA

One approach designed to help teachers build positive student self-concepts and become universally supportive and motivating to *all* students
K–12 in a class is called TESA (Teacher Expectations and Student Achievement). TESA is used primarily as a means of addressing unconscious biases teachers may have toward students that can result in different expectations and achievement. TESA can also be very helpful in shaping classroom practice that supports and motivates students and thereby helps raise their self-esteem.

The program trains teachers in the following classroom strategies:

1. Giving each child an equal chance to respond each day in class
2. Affirming or correcting a student's performance/response
3. Circulating physically among all the children in the class each day
4. Giving individual help to each child as frequently as to any other child
5. Using specific reasons for praising each child's correct response
6. Showing courtesy to students, in and outside class
7. Showing an interest in each student
8. Asking each student questions that search for details and require thought
9. Listening to what each student has to say
10. Touching children in a friendly manner on the shoulder or arm as appropriate
11. Showing feeling toward students, and being accepting of them
12. Attempting to prevent misunderstandings *before* they occur.

Experts agree that spending time and effort helping students develop their self-esteem will pay dividends since self-esteem affects every aspect of human endeavor. It is as significant to school achievement as is intelligence; it certainly is an essential prerequisite to the development of a productive and healthy personality. It is a common factor lacking in school dropouts, drug abusers, and delinquents. It may be the basic factor controlling student behavior. Some consider it the primary basis for the moral decisions people make. Certainly it is a major contributor to both mental and physical health; and it is highly correlated to the manner in which teachers relate to students and students relate to teachers.

# Resources

## Health and Drug Abuse Curricula

"Here's Looking at You, Two," described in *Prevention Plus: Involving Schools, Parents, and the Community in Alcohol and Drug Education*. National Institute on Alcohol Abuse and Alcoholism. Washington, D.C.: Superintendent of Documents, U.S. Government Printing Office, 1984. pp. 2–15.

Materials to help analyze this curriculum and its teacher training component are available from

Comprehensive Health Education Foundation
20832 Pacific Highway South
Seattle, WA 98188
(206) 824-2907

Project Charlie
5701 Normandale Road
Edina, MN 55424
(612) 925-9706

*The Alcohol/Other Drug Risk Reduction Project* Teacher's Guide is available from

Washington Area Council on Alcoholism and
Drug Abuse, Inc.
1232 M Street, NW
Washington, DC 20005
(202) 783-1300

*Amazing Alternatives*

Contact

David M. Murray, Ph.D.
Cheryl L. Perry, Ph.D.
School of Public Health
University of Minnesota
611 Beacon Street, SE
Stadium Gate 27
Minneapolis, MN 55455

Children Are People (K–6 Curriculum)
493 Selby Avenue
St. Paul, MN 55102
(612) 227-4031

Project DARE
Juvenile Division
Los Angeles Police Department
150 North Los Angeles Street
Los Angeles, CA 90028
(213) 485-4856

## Curriculum and Other Program Materials

The *Soozie and Katy* prevention coloring book is available from

U.S. Department of Justice
Drug Enforcement Administration
Washington, DC 20537

*A Story About Feelings Coloring Book*, for children grades K–2, uses cartoon characters from a film, *A Story About Feelings* (color, 10 min., 16 mm or videocassette with teacher guide) to help them gain a clearer understanding of chemical dependency and the role feelings play in their lives. Both are available from

Johnson Institute
510 First Avenue, North
Minneapolis, MN 55403-1607
(612) 341-0435

*Marijuana, A Second Look* can be ordered from the local chapter of the American Lung Association.

American Cancer Society *Smoking Prevention* packet may be ordered from the local chapter of the American Cancer Society.

*Saying No to Alcohol and Drugs* (color, 12 min., 16 mm or videocassette) is available from

Film Fair Communications
10900 Ventura Boulevard
Studio City, CA 91604
(213) 985–0244

*Refusal Skills*

Roberts, Fitzmahan and Associates
9131 California Avenue, SW
Seattle, WA 98136
(206) 932–8409

*This Side Up* is available from NIDA or from the National Clearinghouse for Drug Abuse Information.

## In-Class Activities

*Rappin' About Drugs*

Washington Area Council on Alcoholism and Drug Abuse (WACADA)
1232 M Street, NW
Washington, DC 20005
(202) 783–1300

*Teens in Action* and accompanying materials are available from

National Institute on Drug Abuse
Division of Prevention and Communications
5600 Fishers Lane
Rockville, MD 20857

Information on Takoma Park Junior High School experience is available from

Principal, Takoma Park Junior High School
7611 Piney Branch Road
Silver Spring, MD 20910

*Posters* (free)

Drugs—
National Clearinghouse for Drug Abuse
Information
P.O. Box 416
Kensington, MD 20795
(301) 443-6500

Alcohol—
National Clearinghouse for Alcohol Information
P.O. Box 2345
Rockville, MD 20852
(301) 468-2600

Drinking and Driving—
National Highway Traffic Safety Administration
NTS-11, U.S. Department of Transportation
400 7th Street, SW
Washington, DC 20590
(202) 426-0123

Smoking—
American Lung Association
National Headquarters
1740 Broadway
New York, NY 10019
(212) 245-8000
or from local chapter
American Cancer Society

*Drama*

*Booze* is available from

Marketing Services Department 410
Addiction Research Foundation
33 Russell Street
Toronto, Ontario, Canada M5S2S1

### *Cross-Cultural Materials*

Gaston, Jan. *Cultural Awareness Teaching Techniques*. Brattleboro, Vt.: Prolingua Associates, 1984.

Gaston, Janet. "Cultural Orientation in the English as a Second Language Classroom." In *Beyond Experience*, edited by Donald Batchelder and Elizabeth G. Warner, Brattleboro, Vt.: Experiment Press, 1977. pp. 95, 96.

La Forge, Paul G. *Counseling and Culture in Second Language Acquisition.* Agincourt, Ont.: Dominie Press, 1983.

Available from Council on Interracial Books for Children, Inc., 1841 Broadway, New York, NY 10023–7648:

*Fighting Discrimination*—sound-color filmstrip on strategies for overcoming sexism and racism, grades 5–9.

*The Secret of Goodasme*—sound-color filmstrip on sex and race stereotyping, grades 4–7.

*Unlearning "Indian" Stereotypes*—filmstrip, grades 2 and up.

*Unlearning Asian-American Stereotypes*—filmstrip, elementary and middle school/junior high.

*Unlearning Chicano and Puerto Rican Stereotypes*—filmstrip, grades 5–8.

### *Social Skills in the ESL Classroom*

Akiyama, Carol. *Acceptance to Zeal: Functional Dialogues for Students of English.* New York: Minerva Books, 1981.

Bowers, Barbara, and Godfrey, John. *Decisions*. Agincourt, Ont.: Dominie Press, 1983.

Canario, Jack. *The Big Hassle and Other Plays*. Hayward, Calif.: Janus Book Publishers, 1980.

______. *The Put-Down Pro and Other Plays*. Hayward, Calif.: Janus Book Publishers, 1980.

Day-Garcia, Sharon, and others. *Drink the Winds, Let the Waters Flow Free: American Indians and Recovery from Alcoholism.* Available from Johnson Institute, 510 First Avenue North, Minneapolis, MN 55403–1607.

Doff, Adrian, and Jones, Christopher. *Feelings, A Course in Conversational English for Upper-Intermediate and More Advanced Students.* New York: Cambridge University Press, 1980.

Roderman, W.H. *The Choice and Other Stories.* Hayward, Calif.: Janus Book Publishers, 1980.

## Self-Concept and Social Skills

Canfield, Jack, and Wells, Harold C. *100 Ways To Enhance Self-Concept in the Classroom.* Englewood Cliffs, N.J.: Prentice-Hall, 1976.

Hawkins, J. David, and others. "Childhood Predictors and the Prevention of Adolescent Substance Abuse." In *Etiology of Drug Abuse: Implications for Prevention,* edited by Coryl LaRue Jones and Robert J. Battjes, pp. 75–126. NIDA. Washington, D.C.: Superintendent of Documents, U.S. Government Printing Office, 1985.

Mack, John E., and Ablon, Steven L., eds. *The Development and Sustaining of Self-Esteem in Childhood.* New York: International Universities Press, 1983.

Manatt, Marsha. *Parents, Peers, and Pot.* NIDA. Washington, D.C.: Superintendent of Documents, U.S. Government Printing Office, 1979.

Silvernail, David L. *Developing Positive Student Self-Concept.* 2d ed. Washington, D.C.: National Education Association, 1985.

## *Commercial Programs*

"Building Self-Esteem: A Comprehensive School Program" by Robert Reasoner available from

Self-Esteem, Inc.
3428 Ridgemont Drive
Mountain View, CA 94040
(415) 967–3428

DUSO and Magic Circle materials and guide are available from

Developing Understanding of Self and Others (DUSO)
American Guidance Services
P.O. Box 99
Circle Pines, MN 55014
(612) 786–4343

Magic Circle
Human Development Training Institute
1727 5th Avenue
San Diego, CA 92101

"Skills for Adolescents" (Grades 6–8) and "Skills for Living" (Grades 9–12) are available from

Quest National Center
6655 Sharon Woods Boulevard
Columbus, OH 43229
(614) 882–6400 or 800–446–2700

Schools needing financial support to implement these highly regarded programs should contact their local Lion's Club for assistance.

"Youth Dynamics" available from

Youth Dynamics
P.O. Box 163
Huntington Beach, CA 92647
(714) 894–4529

Simon, Sidney. *I Am Lovable and Capable—A Modern Allegory on the Classical Put-Down*. Allen, Tex.: Argus Communications. (P.O. Box 6000, Allen, TX 75002)

TESA Training Seminar Information (available regionally):

TESA Project Director
Los Angeles County Education Center
9300 East Imperial Highway, Room 246
Downey, CA 90242–2890

# CHAPTER 8

# Parent, Student, and Community Prevention

> I'd get money out of my mom's purse. Then I'd tell her, "I'm going out tonight," and she'd give me $5. And my friends would say to their folks, "We're going out tonight," too. Everyone would get some money, and we'd all put it together. And we'd go get high.
>
> —Amy, age 14

## Parent Power

As with intervention and treatment of student drug and alcohol abuse, prevention activities require more than school involvement in order to be effective. If a clamp down at school moves student drug use to the shopping center parking lot at night or the empty home after school, little is accomplished. Likewise, if children and adolescents are told at school that indiscriminate use of chemical substances may have dire effects, they should hear and see a complementary message at home.

Without parents' full involvement, the efforts of school personnel may not be as effective as possible. Within the last half dozen years, however, parents around the nation have mobilized to fight drug and alcohol abuse. Most of these newly formed groups have urged parents to reassert themselves and take back control of their children's upbringing by following some of these steps:

K–12

- Get together with other parents, particularly those of children with whom your children associate, and find out what is going on among your children and those in the community with regard to drugs.

- Acquaint yourself with the effects, availability, and terminology of drugs.
- Take a firm stand against drug and alcohol use by your children and communicate it clearly and unemotionally to them.
- Agree with your spouse and, if possible, with other parents, upon consistent and fair consequences for violation of rules at home, and support school rules and regulations.
- Keep in touch with other parents, school officials, interested community leaders, and drug treatment providers in the community, preferably through a network or planning group.
- Try to work with others to identify and make available alternatives to drugs for children and adolescents.
- Pay attention to your child's moods, behavior, performance in school, and general demeanor.

The Wisconsin Clearinghouse and the National PTA offer this advice to parents of young children:[57]

K–6

- Teach your children to feel good about themselves by helping them learn to (a) communicate honestly; (b) cooperate with others and take responsibility at an early age; (c) make judgments and decisions; and (d) give and receive unconditional love.
- Provide your children with positive role models by (a) exercising and eating sensibly; (b) maintaining positive, supportive relationships with spouse, children, and friends; (c) recognizing and handling stress in constructive ways; and (d) avoiding the use of drugs and alcohol to relieve tension, stress, unhappiness, and boredom.
- Provide quality time for your children by (a) spending time with each child alone, (b) listening to what your children say, (c) asking your children for their opinions about family problems and decisions, and (d) not talking down to your children.

School staff can support individual parents and parent groups by—

- Keeping them informed of changes in their children's behavior and/or performance at school
- Joining with parents to sponsor parenting skills workshops
- Jointly lobbying local governments to make available recreational and other alternatives to drug use for adolescents in the community
- Generally maintaining regular contact and cooperation with parent and community antidrug abuse groups through faculty and administration representation on the leadership boards of such groups.

## Student-Implemented Activities

Efforts to change existing norms favorable to drug and alcohol use among young people and to decrease some of the widespread acceptance of drug use, particularly alcohol, in society is another way to try to prevent student drug abuse. Efforts to change norms that have included school and community awareness and media campaigns have had some success. Student involvement and leadership of such activities are recent phenomena that seem to have coincided with a decrease in adolescent use of some drugs and less favorable student attitudes toward drug abusers.

### Students Against Driving Drunk (SADD)

9–12

Now found in schools around the nation, SADD started in 1981 in Massachusetts as a student reaction to young people's losing their lives in alcohol-related automobile accidents. SADD's goal is to increase the level of awareness among students about the dangers of drinking and driving. The students themselves, usually with an adult sponsor or adviser, achieve this goal through the use of pamphlets, posters, buttons, bumper stickers, vigils, assemblies, meetings, and workshops. SADD also advocates the use of positive peer pressure to help make drinking and driving unacceptable. It tries to enlist other students in the school by asking them to sign pledges that they will not drink and drive and by asking their parents to also sign contracts. The parents' contract usually stipulates that the student promises not to drink and drive and the parents promise that if the student calls and asks for a ride home, they will provide that ride with no subsequent punishment. The idea is that it is better to save a life by not driving after drinking than to punish people for drinking.

SADD has been credited with saving many teen lives and providing a positive alternative into which kids can channel their energies and talents. The SADD approach, however, is not without its critics. The seemingly tacit approval of teenage drinking, as long as it is not mixed with driving, disturbs many persons who would change the slogan "If you drink, don't drive," to simply "Don't drink." Others find it reasonable, however, when faced with a serious life-threatening problem, to employ a tactic such as SADD does to deal with the immediate problem first—death from drinking and driving. The overall problem of drinking and drug taking should certainly never be forgotten. Ultimately, there must also be concern about changing the popular association between drinking and having a good time. In the meantime, if SADD can save lives, most people have no problem with it as a temporary measure—as long as efforts to discourage teens from any drinking at all also continue. Much of the more recent SADD literature, it should be noted, goes to pains to point out that the purpose of the "Contract for Life" between parents and teenagers is not to endorse drinking, which is illegal for persons under age 21 in most states.

## Peer Counseling

6–12

Peer counseling programs are one of many ways students can help one another. Peer counselors can help those who are having problems, or those who are going through the normal childhood or adolescent stresses and strains and want to confide in someone. Such programs require that teachers and administrators provide support, guidance, and a good deal of training and oversight. Many school systems have used peer counseling programs particularly as an adjunct and supplement to their professional counseling services. Students often will turn to each other and listen to a peer rather than a professional within the school setting when they have a problem or when they need a sounding board. Because peers share a point of view, a language system, similar values and interests, and, because a relationship with a person of the same age lacks the usual control and authority overtones of a relationship with an adult, some students feel more comfortable with this kind of arrangement. Peer counseling programs take this helping relationship that often exists among peers and organize it by providing training for interested students. The training gives them skills in interpersonal communication, decision making, problem solving, and referral procedures. In addition to helping youngsters who may have problems, the peer counselors themselves—those who receive the training—benefit as well. They acquire a set of skills critical to their own self-adjustment and functioning. Many school systems use these programs in grades 7 through 12 but some have also tried them in grades 5 and 6.

Depending upon the specific activities the peer counselors are expected to carry out, their training may be relatively short or somewhat extensive. It may involve simple listening and validation techniques or supervised experience in running discussion groups and making class presentations. At the very least, peer counselors should be able to listen, show support and understanding, and know how to refer troubled classmates to qualified professionals, including counselors, psychologists, and community agencies. Peer counselors generally are not expected to offer solutions, to "preach" to their classmates, to attempt to deliver services, or to work with seriously disturbed youngsters beyond their capabilities and qualifications.

If its limitations are kept clearly in mind and realistic goals and operating procedures are established, peer counseling can be a useful early intervention and prevention approach. Training recovered drug or alcohol abusers as peer counselors may be particularly useful since some kids may resent talking to adults, or even to other students who they think have never used drugs or know little about the drug scene. Recovered abusers, however, should be thoroughly trained and should understand the limitations of their role. Some of these youngsters, because of their missionary zeal to help others, may, if not completely trained, try to accomplish more than they are qualified to undertake.

Depending upon the needs and characteristics of the school, peer counselors may be used in a variety of ways. These include leading group rap sessions; one-to-one counseling with students assigned by the school counselor; making classroom presentations about drugs, decision making, or other social skills; and staffing drop-in centers. In all cases peer counselors should work under the close supervision of a trained counselor and only with youngsters assigned to them.

## Community Prevention Activities

### Community Information and Referral Center

K–12

In one community, the school system and local government joined forces to set up a community drug information and referral center to serve both teachers and parents. The "CARE Center" not only collects and disseminates information on drug and alcohol abuse, education, prevention, and treatment, it also provides many other services, such as the following:

- Functioning as a speakers' bureau for school, parent, and other constituencies
- Enlisting the involvement and material support of local businesses for school- and community anti-drug projects
- Operating a telephone and drop-in referral service for teachers, parents, and students
- Organizing school and community workshops on topics such as "Parenting Skills," "PCP," "Working with Children of Alcoholics," and general awareness-raising seminars
- Functioning as a meeting place for schools, police, courts, social service agencies, and others who work directly with juvenile drug abusers to interact and develop cooperative strategies
- Sponsoring parent awareness, support, and action groups.

Initially, the center was staffed by a coordinator paid by the local government, a secretary paid by the school system, and volunteers. Operating expenses came from businesses and local government funds. More recently, the running of the center has been contracted out to a small private concern in the community, with funding continuing to come from school, government, and business. The center's success is a result of its effectiveness in serving as a focus for the diverse efforts and needs of a variety of constituencies—providers and consumers alike.

## Substance Abuse Prevention and Education Centers (SAPE)

K–12

In Michigan, the State Department of Public Health funds six regional centers, housed in intermediate schools, across the state. Their aim is the prevention of teen substance abuse. The centers' services are available to educators, parents, and students alike:

For Educators:

- Prevention and intervention skills and strategies training
- Program dissemination
- Materials and curriculum distribution
- Current program evaluation
- Curriculum consultation
- Counseling referral

For Parents:

- Effective parenting training

For High School Students:

- Helping to organize SADD chapters, prom and graduation drug-free alternatives
- Summer training on health promotion and substance abuse prevention
- Peer counseling training

## Alliance Against Drugs

In Massachusetts, the Governor's Alliance Against Drugs Campaign focuses on setting up state and local interagency advisory groups that serve as links among police, schools, health agencies, and business. These groups, with seed money from the state, are developing training programs, examining and revising discipline policies, creating curriculum materials, and initiating whatever projects are necessary and appropriate to specific local communities. A major focus of the Massachusetts effort is to concentrate the drug abuse prevention effort from kindergarten through eighth grade. K–8

In New York City, police, like their colleagues in Los Angeles, are in the schools giving substance abuse instruction to fifth and sixth graders. The national PTA, the American Association of School Administrators, the National Association of

Secondary School Principals, the National Education Association, and many other organizations all have encouraged their members to get involved in the fight to combat student drug abuse. And across the nation, communities are mobilizing to fight the problem—preventing it if they can and treating it when they cannot.

## Resources

### Parent Prevention Activities

NIAAA has collected scores of alcohol and drug abuse prevention ideas directly from school and community persons who have tried them with success. Over 60 such ideas with the addresses of the persons who submitted them are described in

*Prevention Plus: Involving Schools, Parents, and the Community in Alcohol and Drug Education*. National Institute on Alcohol Abuse and Alcoholism. Washington, D.C.: Superintendent of Documents, U.S. Government Printing Office, 1984. pp. 253–324.

Also contact
National PTA
Drug Abuse Prevention Project
700 North Rush Street
Chicago, IL 60611
(312) 787-0977

The following provide useful ideas and advice for parents:

Isaacs, Susan, and Fornaciari-Stoll, Suzanne. *Who's in Control: A Parent's Guide to Discipline*. Washington, D.C.: Potomac Press, 1984. (Available from Pacific Institute for Research and Evaluation, 7101 Wisconsin Avenue, Bethesda, MD 20814)

Manatt, Marsha. *Parents, Peers, and Pot II*. NIDA. Washington, D.C.: Superintendent of Documents, U.S. Government Printing Office, 1983.

Meyer, Roberta. *The Parent Connection: How to Communicate with Your Child About Alcohol and Other Drugs.* New York: Franklin Watts Publishing, 1984.

Rose, Marc, and others. *Family Life Skills, Training for Drug Abuse Prevention.* NIDA. Washington, D.C.: Superintendent of Documents, U.S. Government Printing Office, 1984.

## Student-Implemented Activities

Students Against Driving Drunk (SADD)
P.O. Box 800
Marlboro, MA 01752
(617) 481-3568

*Peer Counseling Training Curriculum*
Maryland State Department of Education
200 West Baltimore Street
Baltimore, MD 21201

## Community Prevention Activities

Alliance Against Drugs
Massachusetts Department of Education
Quincy Center Plaza
1385 Hancock Street
Quincy, MA 02169
(617) 770-7500

CARE Center (Community Information and Referral)
200 Park Avenue
Rockville, MD 20850
(301) 279-1555

Substance Abuse Prevention and Education (SAPE) Center
Eaton Intermediate School District
1790 East Packard Highway
Charlotte, MI 48813
(517) 543-5500

# CHAPTER 9

# Treatment Programs for Drug and Alcohol Abuse

It's easy to quit smoking. I've done it a hundred times.
—Mark Twain

Once young people have become dependent on drugs or alcohol, freeing them from this dependence can be extremely difficult. Abusers often do not want to surrender the pleasure of drug use for what they may regard as a harsh reality, and will actively resist treatment. They may pretend to cooperate with the treatment staff, only to return to drug use after release from the program. Teachers and other school personnel should do what they do best—educate children and adolescents. They should not be expected to administer treatment for drug and alcohol dependence. They can help, however, in getting youngsters into treatment and in being supportive of recovered and recovering student drug abusers.

## Types of Treatment

### Professional Programs

Over the past 15 years professional drug treatment programs have proliferated in this country to such an extent that it is now rare to find a community without at least one or two. The most prevalent forms of treatment are (1) drug free, (2) detoxification, and (3) maintenance. The "drug-free" mode treats drug use without medication. Its primary method is counseling. "Detoxification" refers to a treatment of withdrawal from drugs, sometimes with the support of prescribed medication for a limited period with the aim of attracting the abuser into longer-term treatment. If methadone or some other drug substitute is prescribed for longer periods, the treatment mode is called "maintenance." The goal of such programs usually is to eliminate criminal behavior among long-term addicts while establishing a more productive lifestyle.

These basic forms of treatment may be provided in a variety of settings: outpatient or residential; at a hospital or in the community; at a public, nonprofit setting or in a private clinic or office. Certain programs are exclusively for adults while some serve adults and youth. Relatively few serve only young people. Other programs specialize in treating only alcohol abusers or only cocaine or heroin abusers. A few treatment facilities specialize in crisis-oriented emergency services for overdoses or "bad trips" from LSD, PCP, or amphetamines.

One kind of residential, drug-free program is called the "therapeutic community." This kind of program emphasizes persuading adolescents to abandon self-destructive behavior, to come to grips with their problems, and to pursue constructive alternatives to drug use. It uses group therapy, peer confrontation, and counseling to change the values and behaviors that contributed to the drug abuse. Such programs may last from two to eighteen months. Their historical development can be traced to Synanon, established in 1958 by Claude Dederick when he broke off from Alcoholics Anonymous. Programs such as Daytop House, Odyssey House, Phoenix House, Gateway, and Gaudenzia are examples of therapeutic communities. While they have been effective for some youthful addicts, they have been criticized for replacing the youngster's drug dependency with a dependency on the structure and support of the therapeutic community.

Outpatient drug-free programs at hospitals or clinics may feature such strategies as rap sessions, recreational activities, and personal counseling. The average duration of treatment in a day program often is less than six months.

Research studies have shown that each of these treatment programs can produce "substantial improvement in the social functioning and employment of clients and decreases in drug use and criminality."[58] Treatment research studies, however, do not attempt to evaluate "cure" rates. Instead, because drug dependency is now viewed as a chronic disease, much like cardiovascular or arthritic diseases, they measure overall improvement. Few persons are "cured" to the extent that they are no longer at risk for a recurrence of their illness. They tend to follow a relapsing and remitting course, experts tell us, with successive treatments followed by longer periods of remission.[59]

The large majority of such programs, however, serve adult abusers; few, if any, of those studied were for adolescents. The shortage of treatment programs, particularly residential programs, for adolescents is a major problem in many parts of the United States. In many cases, those that do exist for juveniles are private and expensive. Insurance may cover some of the costs, but for those who need treatment and have no insurance or have used up their insurance, the problem may go untreated.

In addition to these formal, structured approaches, professional treatment also is available from individual psychiatrists, psychologists, social workers, and other trained drug abuse therapists who counsel the youngster, the parents, and other family members as well.

Drug-free outpatient treatment is the most likely type for young abusers and those entering treatment for the first time.[60] Regardless of type, however, about half of all persons in treatment discontinue it prematurely, either by dropping out or by being dismissed by the facility for rule violation.[61]

Because behavorial, family, and social problems of adolescent drug abusers are as likely to be the cause as the effect of the drug abuse, some experts believe treatment for adolescents should be oriented toward these problems.[62] Adolescents therefore should not be randomly directed toward various treatment programs; rather, they should be referred based on careful assessment and analysis of their underlying problems. Assignment of a youngster whose problem is primarily one of interpersonal relationships to a treatment program based on theories that ascribe drug abuse to biological or psychological malfunctions may make little sense, and may meet with limited success. In addition, since the longer the treatment the more successful it tends to be,[63] every effort should be made to limit the high treatment dropout rate.

## Self-Help Groups

Unlike the more formal treatment programs described in the preceding pages, most self-help groups are free of charge. The best known and most successful of these groups is Alcoholics Anonymous (AA), a voluntary, worldwide organization that holds regular meetings for alcoholics of all ages, and whose members strive to help each other attain and maintain sobriety.

Recently, AA has been accepting members with drug dependencies other than alcohol, and offshoots of the organization using the same basic approach have sprung up. Two examples are Narcotics Anonymous and Cocaine Anonymous. The companion organizations for the abusers' family members are Al-Anon and now Nar-Anon; the group for teen family members of alcoholics is called Alateen. Other sources of help for parents in confronting and dealing with a child's drug abuse include such parent, peer, and support group offshoots as Toughlove, which uses a "natural consequences" approach to deal with recalcitrant and/or drug-abusing children.

### Other Approaches

In most communities, variations and combinations of these basic approaches can be found. In some communities, including large metropolitan areas, a continuum of drug treatment programs may be available. Occasionally, public school systems conduct their own treatment programs, establishing special schools or programs for drug-abusing students. An example of this approach is the Phoenix School Program in Montgomery County, Maryland. There, students with mild-to-moderate drug problems are allowed to attend a small drug-free day school removed from the influence of drug-using friends. Abstinence is monitored through urinalysis. Besides academics, students receive daily group counseling and drug education. Parents are required to attend regular meetings in the evenings to help them in their interactions with their children at home.

More frequently, however, hospital and other residential programs, such as the therapeutic community type, (a) provide their own schools, (b) contract with the local school system for home instructors, or (c) provide no schooling at all while the youngster is undergoing residential treatment. Many programs now encourage their patients to attend AA or NA meetings both during the treatment and frequently as an aftercare support.

## The School's Role

### Identification

Before treatment of drug or alcohol abuse can begin, the problem must be identified. In general, the earlier the identification, the earlier treatment can begin; and the earlier treatment begins, the better its chances of success. Along with parents, teachers are in a good position to help in identifying the drug problem. Despite the denial, despite the deception, despite the uncertainty and misgivings, teachers and other school personnel must share their concerns about the student's behavior/performance with parents—not once, but repeatedly if necessary. Painfully and reluctantly, but ultimately, the student's family will make that identification—with the help of the school, it will be much sooner.

## Intervention

Depending on the student's stage of drug use, a less restrictive or extreme approach may be enough to put the youngster back on track. The school may be able to help with this kind of early intervention. One school system, for example, assigns students who have been suspended for alcohol or drug use for the first time, or who are suspected of using drugs, to a three-day Drug Education and Awareness Program. On Wednesday, Thursday, and Friday, the program provides a crash course on drugs and their effects, reasons for using drugs, skills for resisting peer pressure, and alternatives to drug use. Parents of students assigned to the program are required to meet with the program staff on the Monday night preceding the three-day session. At this meeting they review the highlights of the program's content, and receive information on the need for vigilance about the drug problem and on community support groups and other resources.

The family, after all, has the primary responsibility for intervention, just as it has for other aspects of the student's drug abuse; the school should not relieve it of that responsibility. Nevertheless, the school may help with early intervention as it does with identification. Many of the prevention activities described in Chapters 6, 7, and 8 are not far removed from early intervention, and in the early stages of experimentation and occasional drug use they may be effective.

Occasionally, schools encounter families that refuse to get help or are themselves so dysfunctional that they are unable to take any kind of constructive action on behalf of their child. At such times the school should refer the case to the child protection unit of the public social service agency. Indeed, referral is mandatory for educators under child abuse and neglect laws in most states.

## Entering Treatment

Even when the student's family has been given an accurate diagnosis of drug dependency and is committed to helping the child solve the problem, obstacles to receiving treatment may still arise. Generally, the more serious the drug abuse problem, the more the student is in need of a structured treatment program.

In many cases, some pressure must be put on the student to enter treatment, particularly a residential or highly structured program. Sometimes the student will progress from less restrictive programs—failing to remain drug free at each—to more restrictive ones. Often the student will be given an ultimatum by parents, or directed by the police or court to enter a program. The school can help by working with parents, social worker, parole officer, case worker, and others to get the youngster into treatment. This may require anything from gentle encouragement from a teacher or counselor with whom the student has a good relationship to threatening to keep the student out of school unless he or she enters treatment. For some students, all options but treatment must be closed before they accept help.

Even persons who argue that treatment will not work if the student does not agree to it admit that few want drug abuse treatment *before* they enter it. Once in a drug-free environment for a week or two, the toxicity level of the student's system starts to recede and the youngster becomes more amenable to the approach. During the initial stages of treatment, however, drug abusers think only of getting out; and they often tell therapists tall tales of abuse and poor treatment at the hands of parents and teachers. At the same time, they may complain bitterly to parents of the mistreatment being inflicted by the treatment program staff. These are natural reactions in adjusting to treatment; they have been observed in many young people undergoing structured treatment programs.

## Aftercare

Completion of a treatment program does not ensure freedom from drug abuse for the rest of one's life; nor is it a solution to all of life's problems. Some youngsters and their families try many programs before they are able to conquer their drug dependence and achieve some stability in their lives and in their relationships with each other. In certain cases, tragically, they never do rise above the drug dependency.

But in those cases where treatment seems effective, there is much to be done to remain drug free and to achieve dominance over the underlying problems that caused or exacerbated the drug abuse. Some experts believe recovered drug abusers will carry a predisposition for drug dependence with them for the rest of their lives; therefore they must continue to be vigilant and abstemious. In any event, most recovered abusers must continue to work on developing their coping skills, their relationships with other family members, and their ability to make new "straight" friends.

Continued therapy, therefore, and continued attendance at AA or NA meetings are recommended long after a youngster has completed a formal treatment program. Parents and other family members also are encouraged to continue in parent support groups or to attend Al-Anon-type meetings. Reintegrating a recovered or recovering drug abuser into school also requires special attention. Unfortunately this is not always provided.

## Reentry

Returning from a long-term residential program to home and school is a particularly difficult transition for a young person. When halfway houses are available, they may help students make the adjustment from treatment center to home. Typically, however, the youngster goes directly back to school—with fear and hope. For many students it is a return to a social situation in which old friends and old expectations create a high-risk situation. At this time, the youngster is particularly vulnerable and in need of encouragement, support, and understanding if the attitudes and skills learned in treatment are to be maintained.

Before the student returns, the treatment program's case worker and/or the parents should contact the school authorities and apprise them of (1) the youngster's date of return, (2) a description of the treatment program's activities and goals, (3) the aftercare program plans, and (4) the date of the discharge conference at the treatment center. The school should assign a case manager (usually a counselor, psychologist, or pupil services worker) to attend the discharge conference and to set up a preliminary reentry conference at the school to develop a transition plan and support system. Such a plan should include the following components:

1. A program schedule that allows for an achievable workload, taking into consideration the possible need for remediation or makeup work, and built-in time for any ongoing outpatient treatment commitments in the late afternoon or evening
2. Extracurricular and/or counseling opportunities such as weekly support group meetings that allow for making new friends and pursuing alternatives to drug use
3. A support team of persons, including a counselor or administrator, non-drug-using students, and a teacher, to whom the returning student can talk at any time of the day as the need arises

4. A recovery contract or plan that prescribes specific consequences in the event a relapse occurs and/or aftercare goals are not met
5. Ongoing consultation with the treatment center aftercare coordinator and the parents.

The basic components of a school-based aftercare program should include the following:

1. Behavior monitoring involving a system of daily or weekly feedback on the student's behavior and academic work
2. Support groups that offer the student an opportunity to meet with other students with similar backgrounds for understanding and encouragement
3. Goals for recovery that may involve school performance and/or attendance, relationships, and sobriety; and that may be monitored while at the same time they give the student a sense of progress and achievement
4. A case manager assigned to assist the student during the reentry process and to coordinate the school's interaction with the treatment center and other parties during the transition period.

On occasion, when the student left school under very negative circumstances, the youngster may be enrolled in a different school. This change protects the student, enabling him or her to start again in a new location without the pressure of old drug-using cronies or a bad reputation among students and faculty.

Whatever school the student returns to, however, it is important that the teachers, counselor, and principal be apprised of the youngster's current drug use and treatment status. Teachers, in particular, need to be aware that a recovering or recovered drug abuser is returning to their class so that they can be sensitive to the student's situation and vigilant for any signs of a problem that may require special assistance. Those who believe teachers should not be told that such students are in their classes in order to protect the youngster from negative stereotyping underestimate the integrity and compassion of teachers. They also overlook the need for constructive in-class monitoring of these youngsters who in the first few months of returning to school are particularly vulnerable to backsliding. At this time they need all the help they can get; confidentiality regulations should not act as a barrier to their getting this help. Classroom teachers are in an exceptionally good position to monitor and report on student behavior. Their vigilance, commitment, and concern, when combined with appropriate knowledge and skill, can save lives.

## Relapse

When, even after the school has done all it can to help implement an aftercare program, a student suffers a relapse and the use of drugs again begins to disrupt classroom teaching and learning, the school must act. A conference among school personnel, parents, student, and treatment center representative should be held to review the student's performance in light of the recovery goals. At this point, the recovery contract, which should have stipulated specific steps to take in such an event, may be invoked.

The conference should decide whether or not to recommend that the student return to treatment or seek other therapy. If that course of action is deemed best, then normal referral procedures should be followed. Just as at the initial referral, students, and sometimes parents, may strongly resist receiving treatment. Unfortunately, it may be necessary for youngsters to undergo treatment more than once, and the school should be just as firm the second time as it was the first.

This, then, brings us almost full circle in the battle to combat student drug and alcohol abuse. The final chapter discusses and puts into perspective the consequences and the future steps in dealing with this problem in the schools.

## Resources

*National Directory of Drug Abuse and Alcoholism Treatment and Prevention Programs.* NIDA and NIAAA. Washington, D.C.: Superintendent of Documents, U.S. Government Printing Office, 1985.

*Comparative Effectiveness of Drug Abuse Treatment Modalities.* NIDA. Washington, D.C.: Superintendent of Documents, U.S. Government Printing Office, 1980.

Johnson, Vernon E. *I'll Quit Tomorrow: A Practical Guide to Alcoholism Treatment.* Rev. ed. New York: Harper and Row, 1973. (Available from the National Council on Alcoholism, 733 Third Ave., New York, NY 10017)

The following films/videos on treatment issues are available from

Gerald T. Rogers Productions
5225 Old Orchard Road, Suite 23
Skokie, IL 60077
(312) 967-8080

*From Now On* (1984)
27 min., color

Three chemically dependent individuals—a young executive, a teenager, and a blue collar worker—are followed through their drug abuse treatment and their struggle to stay drug free. Emphasizes aftercare and the help of the whole family. (High school)

*How to Sabotage Your Treatment*
24 min., color

This film is aimed at patients in treatment programs to help them identify roadblocks they often place in the way of their own recovery. An excellent orientation to what treatment is all about. (High school)

The following treatment and recovery booklets are available from

Johnson Institute
510 First Avenue North
Minneapolis, MN 55403–1607 (1–800–231–5165)

*Chemical Dependency and Recovery Are Family Affairs* (41 pp.)

*Recovery of Chemically Dependent Families* (12 pp.)

*Offbeat and Nontraditional Treatment Methods in Alcoholism* (32 pp.)

*Relapse/Slips: Abstinent Alcoholics Who Return to Drinking* (52 pp.)

For information on representative types of treatment for children and adolescents, contact the following or the local mental health association:

Fairbanks Hospital Inpatient Center
8102 Clearvista Parkway
Indianapolis, IN 46256
(317) 849–8222

Gateway Foundation, Inc.
624 South Michigan Avenue, Suite 1400
Chicago, IL 60605
(312) 663–1130

Jamestown
11550 Jasmine Trail, North
Stillwater, MN 55082
(602) 429–5307

Marworth Adolescent Chemical Dependency Treatment Center
P.O. Box 98
Shawnee-on-Delaware, PA 18356–0098
(717) 563–1112

Phoenix House, Executive Offices
164 West 74th Street
New York, NY 10023
(212) 787–3000

Coordinator, Phoenix School Program
Montgomery County Public Schools
Carver Educational Services Center, Room 230
850 Hungerford Drive
Rockville, MD 20850

Director of Child and Adolescent Services
Psychiatric Institute of Washington, D.C.
4460 MacArthur Boulevard, NW
Washington, DC 20007
(202) 944–3400

Executive Director
Second Genesis Drug Rehabilitation Programs
4720 Montgomery Lane, Suite 502
Bethesda, MD 20814
(301) 656–1545

Director, Straight, Inc.
P.O. Box 848
Marietta, GA 30061
(404) 434–8679

For information on school employees' obligations to report child neglect, see

Tower, Cynthia Crosson. *Child Abuse and Neglect: A Teacher's Handbook for Detection, Reporting, and Classroom Management*. Washington, D.C.: National Education Association, 1984.

For information on a parent support and action group, see

York, Phyllis, and York, David. *Toughlove, A Self-help Manual for Parents Troubled by Teenage Behavior*. Sellersville, Pa.: Community Service Foundation, 1980. (Order from Toughlove, P.O. Box 1069, Doylestown, PA 18901.)

For more information on school awareness training interventions, contact

Substance Abuse Coordinator
Fairfax County Public Schools
Department of Student Services
10310 Layton Hall Drive
Fairfax, VA 22030
(703) 698–7546

For more information on aftercare self-help groups, contact

Alcoholics Anonymous
Box 59
Grand Central Station
New York, NY 10017
(212) 473–6200

Alateen, Al-Anon Family Group Headquarters
P.O. Box 182, Madison Square Station
New York, NY 10159
(212) 481–6565

Nar-Anon Family Groups
P.O. Box 2562
Palos Verdes Peninsula, CA 90274
(213) 547–5800

CHAPTER 10

# What Next?

> Every course of action, including a failure to act at all, has a natural consequence.
>
> —The President's Commission on Organized Crime

Although the rate of student use of most drugs has either declined or remained constant since 1979, an unacceptably large number of young people continue to abuse drugs and alcohol; and the use of such dangerous drugs as cocaine and PCP has actually increased. In addition to deleterious long-term physical effects, the more immediate impact of these chemicals on the mental and emotional development of students can be tragically devastating.

Among the reasons kids take drugs, social pressures—from peers and from family and societal role models—are at the top of the list. Adolescent predisposition toward rebelliousness, nonconformity, and independence also figure prominently.

Student abuse of drugs and alcohol clearly is a problem that belongs to us all—parents, the schools, government, business, and students. Fortunately, our society is mobilizing to fight this scourge. Parents and students alike have organized to combat the problem. Government and business are cracking down on the users of illicit drugs as well as those who traffic in them. Over half of all the Fortune 500 firms reportedly have programs in place to identify drug and alcohol abuse and rehabilitate employees. Many professional athletes and entertainers, sensitive to the bad press they have received for setting a poor example for youth, now go out of their way to present a healthful, drug-free image.

Signs of student drug use, while certainly not infallible, often include falling grades, mood shifts, and estrangement from family and old friends. When a teacher, or other school employee, has cause to suspect a student is abusing drugs, the suggested course of action (see Chapter 5) is to (1) express concern about the youngster's failing grades, moodiness, or other observed behavior; (2) encourage the youngster to seek help and offer to assist in getting that help; (3) if the behavior is extreme or if it persists, notify the parent and similarly express concern over the observed behavior; (4) consult with colleagues about the student and refer the youngster to appropriate staff; and (5) participate in the intervention program if appropriate.

Specific steps for attacking the drug problem and identifying the roles staff members should play are best laid out in comprehensive school policies and regulations. This removes the uncertainty from the situation and allows each individual to know what role he/she may properly play and which procedure to employ. Questions such as who should call the parent or whether to hold a student's confession in confidence are then answered clearly.

Training staff, assessing the scope of the problem, enforcing rules, and forming coalitions with parents, students, and the community-at-large are also important steps in attacking the problem. The major components of the school's antidrug effort, however, are early intervention and prevention activities. Although no one prevention approach has proven to be totally effective, programs based on the reasons students take drugs, such as social pressures, hold the most promise. When prevention and early intervention fail, schools should be prepared to refer students to professional drug treatment, and to support the student's reentry and transition back to school after treatment.

The following checklist may be useful in determining if a school has touched all the important bases and in identifying any missing elements:

1. Has the school developed a cooperative relationship with community groups and organizations active (or capable of becoming active) in the fight against student drug and alcohol abuse?

2. Is the school strictly enforcing rules on drug use, possession, and distribution?
3. Is the school integrating drug abuse information and needed social skills into the curriculum, especially in upper elementary and junior high schools; and are school staff adopting new research-based health education curricula and extending their use to begin in the primary grades?
4. Is the school training faculty and staff on the effects of drugs, and the skills needed to recognize and appropriately confront the problem?
5. Is the school addressing associated and related destructive behaviors—abuse, eating disorders, delinquency, chronic absenteeism, suicide?
6. Is the school attempting to change norms through the use of positive peer pressure, and by supporting student antidrug activists?
7. Does the school have a fully developed set of prevention and intervention strategies in place?
8. Has the school developed, revised, and publicized school drug policies to students, parents, and the community?
9. Has the school assigned specific responsibility and authority, and provided adequate resources for organizing, implementing, and evaluating its antidrug efforts?

This last question is particularly important. It has to do, in many instances, with why some schools' antidrug efforts are effective and ongoing and others have little or no impact and fade because of neglect and loss of interest when a key staff member leaves. The answer to why some programs work and last and others do not is usually related to one or more of the following reasons:

- Policies and rules are either not implemented or are implemented inconsistently.
- Program responsibilities and duties are expected to be undertaken without proper budget and staff.

- Overall responsibility and authority are either assigned to too many individuals or to no one in particular.

School drug prevention and intervention programs that work and last have one person in charge, their own budget and staff resources, and well-thought-out, consistently implemented policies and rules. They also tend to be characterized by dedication and enthusiasm on the part of those working with them, support from the school's leadership, the trust of school staff and community alike, and consistency from one school to another within the same school district.

Does this mean that a school that cannot have a full-blown program should not bother to have any? It does not. Different schools across the nation have adopted very different policies and rules. Some have been comprehensive and far-reaching in scope; others have concentrated on narrower goals. Each school must look at its own particular situation—its student body, its staff, its community—and decide for itself how it will deal with the problem of student drug and alcohol abuse.

Throughout this book, I have attempted to stress the importance of ownership and action and to present useful information and resources with which to act. Now it is up to the readers. What you decide to do is important; but it is not nearly as important as the decision you make—*to do something*.

# Appendices

# Appendix A

## State Drug Abuse Prevention Agencies

**Alabama**
Drug Abuse Program Section
Division of Alcoholism and Drug Abuse
Department of Mental Health
145 Molton Street
Montgomery, AL 36104

**Alaska**
Office of Drug Abuse
Dept. of Health & Social Services
Pouch H-01D
Juneau, AK 99801

**Arizona**
Drug Abuse Programs
Division of Behavioral Health Services
Department of Health Services
2500 East Van Buren
Phoenix, AZ 85008

**Arkansas**
Office of Drug and Alcohol Abuse Prevention
Dept. of Social & Rehab. Services
1515 Building
1515 West 7th
Little Rock, AR 72203

**California**
California Department of Health
Substance Abuse Division
Room 1592, 744 P Street
Sacramento, CA 95814

**Colorado**
Alcohol & Drug Abuse Division
Department of Health
4210 East 11th Avenue
Denver, CO 80220

**Connecticut**
Connecticut Alcohol and Drug Council
Department of Mental Health
90 Washington Street
Hartford, CT 06115

**Delaware**
Bureau of Substance Abuse
Governor Bacon Health Center
Cottage #8
Delaware City, DE 19706

**Florida**
Bureau of Drug Abuse Prevention
Division of Mental Health
Dept. of Health & Rehab. Services
1317 Winewood Blvd.
Tallahassee, FL 32301

**Georgia**
Alcohol and Drug Abuse Section
Div. of Mental Health & Retardation
Department of Human Resources
618 Ponce De Leon Avenue, N.E.
Atlanta, GA 30308

**Hawaii**
Alcohol and Drug Abuse Branch
Department of Health
1270 Queen Emma Street, Room 404
Honolulu, HI 96813

**Idaho**
Bureau of Substance Abuse
Division of Community Rehabilitation
Department of Health and Welfare
LBJ Building, Room 327
Boise, ID 83720

**Illinois**
Dangerous Drugs Commission
300 North State Street, 15th Floor
Chicago, IL 60610

**Indiana**
Division of Addiction Services
Department of Mental Health
5 Indiana Square
Indianapolis, IN 46204

**Iowa**
Iowa Drug Abuse Authority
615 East 14th Street
Des Moines, IA 50319

**Kansas**
Drug Abuse Unit
Dept. of Social and Rehab. Services
2700 W. 6th Street, Biddle Bldg.
Topeka, KS 66608

**Louisiana**
Bureau of Substance Abuse
Division of Hospitals
Louisiana Health and Human Resource Administration
Weber Building, 7th Floor
Baton Rouge, LA 70801

**Maine**
Office of Alcoholism and Drug Abuse Prevention
Bureau of Rehabilitation
32 Winthrop Street
Augusta, ME 04330

**Maryland**
Drug Abuse Administration
Dept. of Health & Mental Hygiene
Herbert O'Conor Office Building
201 W. Preston Street
Baltimore, MD 21201

**Massachusetts**
Division of Drug Rehabilitation
Department of Mental Health
190 Portland Street
Boston, MA 02114

**Michigan**
Office of Substance Abuse Services
3500 North Logan Street
P.O. Box 30035
Lansing, MI 48909

**Minnesota**
Drug and Alcohol Authority
Chemical Dependency Division
Dept. of Public Welfare
402 Metro Square Building
St. Paul, MN 55101

**Mississippi**
Division of Drug Misuse
Department of Mental Health
1001 Lee State Office Building
Jackson, MS 39201

**Missouri**
Division of Alcoholism & Drug Abuse
Department of Mental Health
2002 Missouri Blvd.
Jefferson City, MO 65101

**Montana**
Addictive Diseases Division
Department of Institutions

1539 11th Avenue
Helena, MT 59601

**Nebraska**
Nebraska Commission on Drugs
P.O. Box 94726
State Capitol Building
Lincoln, NE 68509

**Nevada**
Bureau of Alcohol & Drug Abuse
Rehabilitation Division
Department of Human Resources
505 East King Street
Carson City, NV 89710

**New Hampshire**
Office of Drug Abuse Prevention
3 Capital Street, Room 405
Concord, NH 03301

**New Jersey**
Division of Narcotic and Drug Abuse Control
Department of Health
541 East State Street
Trenton, NJ 08609

**New Mexico**
Drug Abuse Agency
Department of Hospitals & Institutions
113 Washington
Santa Fe, NM 87501

**New York**
Office of Drug Abuse Services
Executive Park South
Albany, NY 12203

**North Carolina**
North Carolina Drug Commission
Box 19324
Raleigh, NC 27609

**North Dakota**
Division of Alcoholism and Drug Abuse
Department of Health
909 Basin Avenue
Bismarck, ND 58505

**Ohio**
Ohio Bureau of Drug Abuse
Division of Mental Health
Department of Mental Health and Mental Retardation
65 S. Front Street, Room 211
Columbus, OH 43215

## Oklahoma
Division of Drug Abuse Services
Department of Mental Health
P.O. Box 53277, Capitol Station
Oklahoma City, OK 73105

## Oregon
Programs for Alcohol and Drug Problems
Mental Health Division
Department of Human Resources
2575 Bittern Street, N.E.
Salem, OR 97310

## Pennsylvania
Governor's Council on Drug and Alcohol Abuse
Riverside Office Center
Building #1, Suite N
1101 North Front Street
Harrisburg, PA 17110

## Rhode Island
Rhode Island Drug Abuse Program
Department of Mental Health and Retardation and Hospitals
303 General Hospital
Rhode Island Medical Center
Cranston, RI 02920

## South Carolina
South Carolina Commission on Alcohol and Drug Abuse
3700 Forest Drive
P.O. Box 4616
Columbia, SC 29240

## South Dakota
Division of Drugs and Substance Control
Department of Health
Joe Foss Building
Pierre, SD 57501

## Tennessee
Alcohol and Drug Abuse Section
Department of Mental Health
501 Union Street, 4th Floor
Nashville, TN 37219

## Texas
Drug Abuse Division
Department of Community Affairs
Box 13166, Capitol Station
Austin, TX 78711

## Utah
Division of Alcoholism and Drugs
554 South 300 East
Salt Lake City, UT 84111

### Vermont
Alcohol and Drug Abuse Division
Department of Social & Rehab. Services
State Office Building
Montpelier, VT 05602

### Virginia
Department of Mental Health/Mental Retardation
Division of Substance Abuse Control
Commonwealth of Virginia
P.O. Box 1797
Richmond, VA 23214

### Washington
Office of Drug Abuse Prevention
Community Services Division
DSHS, OB-43E
Olympia, WA 98504

### West Virginia
Division of Alcoholism and Drug Abuse
Department of Mental Health
1800 Washington Street, East
Charleston, WV 25305

### Wisconsin
Bureau of Alcohol & Other Drug Abuse
Division of Mental Hygiene
Department of Health and Social Services
One West Wilson Street, Room 523
Madison, WI 53702

### Wyoming
Drug Abuse Programs
State Office Building West
Cheyenne, WY 82001

# Appendix B

## Additional Organizations to Contact for Help, Information, and Materials

Alateen, Al-Anon Family Group Headquarters, Inc.
P.O. Box 182
Madison Square Station
New York, NY 10159
(212) 481-6565

Alcoholics Anonymous
General Service Office
P.O. Box 459

Grand Central Station
New York, NY 10163
(212) 686-1100

American Automobile Association (AAA)
Traffic Safety Department
Falls Church, VA 22047
(703) 222-5000

American Cancer Society
777 Third Avenue
New York, NY 10017
(212) 371-2900

American Council for Drug Education
5820 Hubbard Drive
Rockville, MD 20852
(301) 984-5700

American Lung Association
1740 Broadway
New York, NY 10019
(212) 245-8000

National Association for Children of Alcoholics
31706 Coast Highway, Suite 201
South Laguna, CA 92677

National Clearinghouse for Alcohol Information
P.O. Box 2345
Rockville, MD 20852

National Clearinghouse for Drug Abuse Information
P.O. Box 416
Kensington, MD 20795
800-638-2045 (National)
800-492-2948 (Maryland)

National Council on Alcoholism
733 Third Avenue
New York, NY 10017

National Federation of Parents for Drug-Free Youth
1820 Franwall Avenue
Silver Spring, MD 20902
(301) 649-7100

National Highway Traffic Safety Administration
Office of Alcohol Countermeasures
NTS 21
400 Seventh Street, SW
Washington, DC 20590

National Institute on Drug Abuse (NIDA)
5600 Fishers Lane
Rockville, MD 20857
(301) 443-6245

National School Safety Center
7311 Greenhaven Drive
Sacramento, CA 95831
(916) 427–4600

Parents' Resource Institute for Drug Education (PRIDE)
100 Edgewood Avenue, Suite 1216
Atlanta, GA 30303
800–241–7946
(404) 658–2548

Center for Community Change
100 Wisconsin Avenue, NW
Washington, DC 20007

Linking community groups with community development techniques is the focus of the Center for Community Change. The Center concentrates on the problems facing low-income communities and provides training in strategies and advocacy.

Center for Multi-Cultural Awareness (CMA)
2924 Columbia Pike
Arlington, VA 22204

A project of the National Institute on Drug Abuse (NIDA), operated by Development Associates, CMA is a resource center for Black, Native American, Asian-American, Puerto Rican, Mexican-American, and other Hispanic communities. It identifies, develops, and adopts culturally relevant materials for drug abuse prevention, and provides technical planning assistance to state agencies, as well as assistance to local programs within minority communities. The Center also has expertise in networking and coalition building to offer community groups.

U.S. Department of Education
Black Concerns Staff
Hubert Humphrey Building
200 Independence Avenue, SW
Washington, DC 20201

The Black Concerns Staff of DOE has current information available on network building and federal funding.

National Black Alcoholism Council (NBAC)
United Methodist Building
100 Maryland Avenue, NE
Washington, DC 20002

NBAC is a newly formed organization dedicated to working with Black people and the devastation of alcoholism in Black communities. The Council may be of assistance to community workers engaged in treatment, prevention, public policy, research, and planning.

National Center for Alcohol Education (NCAE)
1601 North Kent Street
Arlington, VA 22209

The NCAE offers training packages in programming, community resources, planning, maintaining a volunteer program, and training the youth worker in an alcohol service agency. Of particular interest is a prevention kit available for Black communities, entitled "Ounce of Prevention."

National Council on Alcoholism (NCA)
Minority Program
733 Third Avenue
New York, NY 10017

NCA provides technical assistance in program planning and evaluation for minority groups. It distributes literature on alcohol and minorities, and maintains a list of minority consultants and projects to assist program planners.

National Parent Teacher Association (PTA)
Alcohol Education Project
700 North Rush Street
Chicago, IL 60611

The National PTA has a history of working with parents and youth on issues around youthful drug abuse and drinking. A series of four two-hour workshops designed for parents to help children make informed decisions about drinking is available from the Alcohol Education Project.

National Youth Work Alliance (NYWA)
1346 Connecticut Avenue, NW
Washington, DC 20036

NYWA is a reference and information service for youth workers and program developers. It publishes resource materials and a newsletter, *Youth Alternatives*. It also hosts an Annual National Youth Workers Conference and various training programs on specific topics of interest to youth workers.

Pyramid Project
7101 Wisconsin Avenue, Suite 1006
Bethesda, MD 20014

Pyramid West
3746 Mt. Diablo Blvd., Suite 200
Lafayette, CA 94549

Pyramid Project is a resource-sharing network in the field of primary drug abuse prevention funded by the Prevention Branch of the National Institute on Drug Abuse (NIDA), Division of Resource Development. It provides assistance and information on community management and staff development; prevention strategies, media, needs assessment, and community organizations; research and evaluation; prevention curricula; funding resources; and training. Pyramid acts as a consultant in directly addressing specific problems facing an agency or identifies other appropriate individuals/organizations that may offer consultant services to the agency.

# Appendix C

## High School Senior Drug Use: 1975–1985

The following tables show the percentage of high school seniors from the classes of 1975 through 1985 who have used drugs of abuse. These numbers were gathered in annual nationwide surveys conducted for the National Institute on Drug Abuse by the University of Michigan Institute for Social Research. The 1985 survey involved more than 16,000 high school seniors from public and private schools.

**Table 1**

**Used in Last Year**

| | | | | | | Class of | | | | | |
|---|---|---|---|---|---|---|---|---|---|---|---|
| | '75 | '76 | '77 | '78 | '79 | '80 | '81 | '82 | '83 | '84 | '85 |
| Marijuana/Hashish | 40% | 45% | 48% | 50% | 51% | 49% | 46% | 44% | 42% | 40% | 41% |
| Inhalants | NA | NA | NA | NA | 9 | 8 | 6 | 7 | 7 | 8 | 7 |
| Amyl & Butyl Nitrites | NA | NA | NA | NA | 7 | 6 | 4 | 4 | 4 | 4 | 4 |
| Hallucinogens | NA | NA | NA | NA | 13 | 11 | 10 | 9 | 9 | 8 | 8 |
| LSD | 7 | 6 | 6 | 6 | 7 | 7 | 7 | 6 | 5 | 5 | 4 |
| PCP | NA | NA | NA | NA | 7 | 4 | 3 | 2 | 3 | 2 | 3 |
| Cocaine | 6 | 6 | 7 | 9 | 12 | 12 | 12 | 12 | 11 | 12 | 13 |
| Heroin | 1 | 1 | 1 | 1 | 1 | 1 | 1 | 1 | 1 | 1 | 1 |
| Other Opiates | 6 | 6 | 6 | 6 | 6 | 6 | 6 | 5 | 5 | 5 | 6 |
| Stimulants | NA | NA | NA | NA | NA | NA | NA | 20 | 18 | 18 | 16 |
| Sedatives | 12 | 11 | 11 | 10 | 10 | 10 | 11 | 9 | 8 | 7 | 6 |
| Barbiturates | 11 | 10 | 9 | 8 | 8 | 7 | 7 | 6 | 5 | 5 | 5 |
| Methaqualone | 5 | 5 | 5 | 5 | 6 | 7 | 8 | 7 | 5 | 4 | 3 |
| Tranquilizers | 11 | 10 | 11 | 10 | 10 | 9 | 8 | 7 | 7 | 6 | 6 |
| Alcohol | 85 | 86 | 87 | 88 | 88 | 88 | 87 | 87 | 87 | 86 | 86 |
| Cigarettes | NA | NA | NA | NA | NA | NA | NA | NA | NA | NA | NA |

**Table 2**

**Used in Past Month**

| | | | | | | Class of | | | | | |
|---|---|---|---|---|---|---|---|---|---|---|---|
| | '75 | '76 | '77 | '78 | '79 | '80 | '81 | '82 | '83 | '84 | '85 |
| Marijuana/Hashish | 27% | 32% | 35% | 37% | 37% | 34% | 32% | 29% | 27% | 25% | 26% |
| Inhalants | NA | NA | NA | NA | 3 | 3 | 2 | 3 | 3 | 3 | 3 |
| Amyl & Butyl Nitrites | NA | NA | NA | NA | 2 | 2 | 1 | 1 | 1 | 1 | 2 |
| Hallucinogens | NA | NA | NA | NA | 6 | 4 | 4 | 4 | 4 | 4 | 4 |
| LSD | 2 | 2 | 2 | 2 | 2 | 2 | 3 | 2 | 2 | 2 | 2 |
| PCP | NA | NA | NA | NA | 2 | 1 | 1 | 1 | 1 | 1 | 2 |
| Cocaine | 2 | 2 | 3 | 4 | 6 | 5 | 6 | 5 | 5 | 6 | 7 |
| Heroin | * | * | * | * | * | * | * | * | * | * | * |
| Other Opiates | 2 | 2 | 3 | 2 | 2 | 2 | 2 | 2 | 2 | 2 | 2 |
| Stimulants | NA | NA | NA | NA | NA | NA | NA | 11 | 9 | 8 | 7 |
| Sedatives | 5 | 5 | 5 | 4 | 4 | 5 | 5 | 3 | 3 | 2 | 2 |
| Barbiturates | 5 | 4 | 4 | 3 | 3 | 3 | 3 | 2 | 2 | 2 | 2 |
| Methaqualone | 2 | 2 | 2 | 2 | 2 | 3 | 3 | 2 | 2 | 1 | 1 |
| Tranquilizers | 4 | 4 | 5 | 3 | 4 | 3 | 3 | 2 | 3 | 2 | 2 |
| Alcohol | 68 | 68 | 71 | 72 | 72 | 72 | 71 | 70 | 69 | 67 | 66 |
| Cigarettes | 37 | 39 | 38 | 37 | 34 | 31 | 29 | 30 | 30 | 29 | 30 |

## Table 3

### Daily Users

| | '75 | '76 | '77 | '78 | '79 | Class of '80 | '81 | '82 | '83 | '84 | '85 |
|---|---|---|---|---|---|---|---|---|---|---|---|
| Marijuana/Hashish | 6.0% | 8.0% | 9.1% | 10.7% | 10.3% | 9.1% | 7.0% | 6.3% | 5.5% | 5.0% | 4.9% |
| Inhalants | NA | NA | NA | NA | 0.1 | 0.2 | 0.2 | 0.2 | 0.2 | 0.2 | 0.4 |
| Amyl & Butyl Nitrites | NA | NA | NA | NA | 0.0 | 0.1 | 0.1 | 0.0 | 0.2 | 0.1 | 0.3 |
| Hallucinogens | NA | NA | NA | NA | 0.2 | 0.2 | 0.1 | 0.2 | 0.2 | 0.2 | 0.3 |
| LSD | 0.0 | 0.0 | 0.0 | 0.0 | 0.0 | 0.0 | 0.1 | 0.0 | 0.1 | 0.1 | 0.1 |
| PCP | NA | NA | NA | NA | 0.1 | 0.1 | 0.1 | 0.1 | 0.1 | 0.1 | 0.3 |
| Cocaine | 0.1 | 0.1 | 0.1 | 0.1 | 0.2 | 0.2 | 0.3 | 0.2 | 0.2 | 0.2 | 0.4 |
| Heroin | 0.1 | 0.0 | 0.0 | 0.0 | 0.0 | 0.0 | 0.0 | 0.0 | 0.1 | 0.0 | 0.0 |
| Other Opiates | 0.1 | 0.1 | 0.2 | 0.1 | 0.0 | 0.1 | 0.1 | 0.1 | 0.1 | 0.1 | 0.1 |
| Stimulants | NA | NA | NA | NA | NA | NA | NA | 0.7 | 0.8 | 0.6 | 0.4 |
| Sedatives | 0.3 | 0.2 | 0.2 | 0.2 | 0.1 | 0.2 | 0.2 | 0.2 | 0.2 | 0.1 | 0.1 |
| Barbiturates | 0.1 | 0.1 | 0.2 | 0.1 | 0.0 | 0.1 | 0.1 | 0.1 | 0.1 | 0.0 | 0.1 |
| Methaqualone | 0.0 | 0.0 | 0.0 | 0.0 | 0.0 | 0.1 | 0.1 | 0.1 | 0.0 | 0.0 | 0.0 |
| Tranquilizers | 0.1 | 0.2 | 0.3 | 0.1 | 0.1 | 0.1 | 0.1 | 0.1 | 0.1 | 0.1 | 0.0 |
| Alcohol | 5.7 | 5.6 | 6.1 | 5.7 | 6.9 | 6.0 | 6.0 | 5.7 | 5.5 | 4.8 | 5.0 |
| Cigarettes | 26.9 | 28.8 | 28.8 | 27.5 | 25.4 | 21.3 | 20.3 | 21.1 | 21.2 | 18.7 | 19.5 |

NA indicates data not available
*Indicates less than .5%

**Terms:**

*Used in Last Year:* Used at least once in the 12 months prior to survey.

*Used in Past Month:* Used at least once in the 30 days prior to survey.

*Daily Users:* Used 20 or more times in the month prior to survey.

Source: National Institute on Drug Abuse, *Monitoring the Future Study, 1985* (Washington, D.C.: Superintendent of Documents, U.S. Government Printing Office, 1986).

# Appendix D

## School Policy Statement*

The Rights of Students Seeking Help for Alcohol and Other Drug Problems Must Be Protected as Proscribed by Law.

It is important that educators serve in a helping role to students who are seeking to overcome alcohol/drug abuse and/or dependency. Public School Law 7–410 encourages students to ask educators for help with drug abuse problems. The law protects the student and educator from disclosing any information discussed. Furthermore, Bylaw 13A.08.02, Individual Student Records, provides additional protection to students concerning information recorded in their school records. Public Law 93.579 (Title V USC Sec. 552A—the Buckley Amendment) also protects the confidentiality of school records. However, this law applies only to records kept by the school. Any records transferred to an outside agency can be subpoenaed. However, this should not discourage students from seeking help. . . .

*Teacher Involvement*

A teacher, administrator, or counselor may respond to a student seeking help with a chemical dependency or abuse problem and cannot be compelled to use the information in a disciplinary manner. All school personnel should be aware of the distinction between students seeking help and those who are violating the law. All incidents regarding possession or distribution of alcohol/drugs should be reported by school personnel to the principal. This rule may not apply if the student seeks help for his/her drug problem. An educator who suspects alcohol/drug use may approach the student with an offer to help, but the confidentiality law applies only if the student then asks for help.

In most instances, professional help from alcohol/drug treatment agencies should also be sought. Each educator should be aware of the professional help available to alcohol/drug involved youth and should make use of these resources when needed.

As with any sensitive problem, any additional help should be sought without destroying the confidential relationship between student and educator. Students should know that there is a continuing concern on the part of the educator even when other resources are pursued. The impact of

*Selections from *School Policy: Alcohol and Other Drugs*, Maryland State Department of Education, 1982. Reprinted with permission.

all efforts should be to constantly reinforce the help-seeking behavior of students with drug problems. If a student enlists the assistance of an educator, it is important that the educator should ask the student about any past or current counseling. Further suggestions regarding teacher/student counseling are found in the section entitled "The Helping Relationship."

### *Guidelines for Drug Abuse Counseling*

Guidelines for drug abuse counseling were adopted by the Maryland State Board of Education as Resolution No. 1971–50. They should be used as basic guidelines by educators counseling students. The full text of the guidelines is included here. While it is established that educators who meet with students are under no legal duty to inform the parents about a student's visit or drug abuse problem, every effort should be made to encourage the student to involve his/her parents in the problem.

### *General Professional Guidelines*[1]

I. Every case in which a student seeks counseling or information from a professional educator to overcome drug abuse must be handled on an individual basis, which will depend upon the nature and particulars of the subject case. In determining what procedures might be appropriate, the educator from whom such information is sought should consider the following factors:
   - A. Age of student
   - B. Type of drug
   - C. Intensity of involvement
   - D. Sincerity of student and willingness to undertake appropriate treatment
   - E. Resources available
   - F. Parental involvement

II. As in any good helping relationship, the educator at the earliest appropriate time is encouraged to discuss the availability of other resources, his/her professional limitations, and the desirability of parental involvement. Decisions to include parents should be made *jointly by the student and educator*, unless in the judgment of the educator, the mental or physical health of the child is immediately and dangerously threatened.

III. The law on confidentiality places no duty on the part of educators to inform parents, administrators, or law enforcement personnel of the identity of students seeking help for overcoming drug abuse problems.

[1]State Board Publication (1971). MSBE Resolution No. 1971–50.

IV. While confidentiality is a major force in enhancing help-seeking by current or potential drug abusers, educators are cautioned to obtain professional medical advice or to refer the student to the appropriate available medical facility if there is an immediate and dangerous threat to the student's physical or mental health. As in the performance of any professional role, failure to act reasonably in a drug counseling case may subject the educator to civil liability.

V. Examples of immediate and dangerous threats to a student's health are loss of consciousness, severe intoxication, inability to communicate coherently, or threat of suicide.

VI. When an educator comes into possession of a substance suspected to be a drug, the material should be placed in the custody of the principal who will contact the appropriate law enforcement agency. When such suspected substances are received by any member of the school faculty, the following steps should be taken:

A. Immediately place the substance in an envelope or other container and label the container with the date, time, and circumstances. NOTE: When such substances are acquired by an educator *during a counseling/information-seeking conference*, the name of the *student should not be indicated.* In all other instances where an educator comes into possession of drugs, the name of the individual should be carefully noted.

B. Do not taste the suspected substance under any circumstances.

C. At the earliest opportunity, turn the material over to the principal who in turn will keep it under lock and key.

D. The principal or person holding the substance in every case should notify the local or state police and turn over all substances.

E. The principal should give the educator a receipt stating the quantity of the drug. It should be remembered that no authority has been given to any school personnel to possess any prohibited drug or paraphernalia except during the transfer to proper authorities.

VII. Helping role contacts with students seeking to overcome a drug problem should be held on school premises whenever possible.

VIII. If an educator feels incapable of providing adequate help for a student or feels his/her counseling can no longer benefit the student, the educator and student should cooperatively seek additional professional help from available sources.

IX. Any written information pertaining to or about the information seeking/counseling session should be regarded as the personal notes of the educator. No record should be kept in any official school file or folder.

X. All educators should have access to a list of local resources where students with drug problems may be referred for help. (It would also be beneficial to have in each school a drug resource person who could act as a sharing person to aid an educator involved in counseling a drug-involved student.)

XI. In the general classroom situation, teachers should not attempt to diagnose symptoms of drug abuse. Because of the difficulty of determining such symptoms, it is suggested that any time a student is physically or mentally incapable of functioning properly in class, he/she should be sent to the school health facility where the usual school health referral procedures should be followed.

### *The Helping Relationship*

Any educator—or almost anyone associated with the educational process—is often thrust suddenly into the "helping" role when interacting with young people today. The "generation gap" is accentuated by such factors as the nature of youth's discontent and the means by which it is expressed. Thus, philosophically, the adult and youth may find themselves hopelessly opposed as each says the other will "never understand." Their positions become emotionally polarized as the adult says, "Get out and never come back," and the youth says, "Okay." Thereafter, each retreats to the respective peer group and justifies action thus taken. This prototype of interaction occurs daily in homes and schools all over the state. Too often the nature of the apparently insoluble conflict has to do with drug abuse.

Youth today, by virtue of their sophistication, have an uncanny accuracy for directing their plea for help to sympathetic adults. This, of course, does not imply sincerity on the part of either participant. The adult who feels the need to be liked by all students should be aware that behavior resulting from this need to be liked may not be in the student's best interest.

The nature of the counseling process is the simultaneous differentiation of roles and merging of goals between the two participants. It is a microspectrum of parenthood, but is presumably carried out between a mature adult and a youth who are not burdened by adverse emotional investment in each other. The process is destined to fail if the youth's behavior is persistently justified at the expense of sincere introspection and if the adult agrees with this line of reasoning.

Students ask for personal help in drug matters in many ways. Sometimes the request is blunt: "I'm scared. I'm hooked on drug X." But more often the request is worded, "I know this guy _________," or "What would happen if _________." Most often the questions come to the educator piecemeal as the student tests the response. Thus it is wise to employ similar rhetorical and abstract techniques in questioning and responding as those used by the student. For example, even if both teacher and student know that they are really talking about the student, it should be the student who says, "That other guy I've been telling you about is really me." The educator should never forget that the diplomatic handling of this initial, frustrating, tentative contact with the youngster may be life saving and that the youngster has chosen the educator in lieu of all other adults including the youth's parents.

The following are offered as very general guidelines for individual counseling with students who seek your help in matters related to drug abuse. They are not intended to preempt your personal experience or judgment.

I. *Initial Contact.* Some students may be evasive, talk in the third person, begin with a safe topic and generally test the educator for some indication of interest, sincerity, strength and drug awareness. Others may be blunt and shocking in their first contact, but they may also be testing for the above conditions.

II. *Shock Material.* Chronic drug-involved students sometimes attempt to shock the educator with a discussion of material which may seem initially overwhelming or appalling. Such material might include criminal behavior, severe depression, parental punishment, prostitution, or homosexual behavior. Educators who find themselves unable to evaluate the real versus exaggerated meaning of such revelations of a student should obtain the advice of a local resource person.

Confidentiality should be maintained despite this outside-the-relationship contact. It is desirable that the student be made aware of the specific contact or be generally aware that the educator is involved in professional sharing of material discussed.

III. *Third-Person Reference.* A student who refers to a "friend's" drug problem may be talking about himself/herself or may truly be talking about a friend and not want to be identified. If talking about a real friend, the student should be told of the educator's position relative to the existing legislative provisions, i.e., protection of divulged information, and requested to pass this legal information on to the drug-involved friend.

IV. *Referral.* No educator need feel locked into the role of confidential adviser to a student who asks for help in matters of drug abuse. Should a teacher, counselor, or administrator feel unable to help a youngster, the educator should attempt to refer the requesting student to a colleague or other available professional. After a helping relationship has begun, both the educator and the student have the option to cease further sessions together. At that point, the educator may suggest an appropriate referral. If there appears to be an imminent threat to the physical or mental health of the student and the relationship has been terminated, a report must be made to some responsible adult such as a parent, physician, or school administrator who can provide definitive help. It is desirable to inform the student of this.

V. *Why Me?* The crucial ingredient in counseling is a trusting relationship. The student has generally chosen the educator as an adult adviser, and the reasons for that choice are usually unknown to both. The educator may have been presented as an authority by a fellow student or a colleague. The educator may have shown understanding in a personal or class discussion. The educator's appearance may remind the student of a trusted (or vulnerable) person previously known or the educator's own feelings for the student may have invited the confidence. Whatever the reasons for getting together in the one-to-one counseling role, the educator must take a careful look at those reasons. The initial question for a prospective teacher/counselor has to be "Why me?"

VI. *Counseling Contract.* Thereafter, the educator must deal with the counseling contract. There has to be tactful honesty. This need not be so negative as, "I'm not sure that you've come to the right person, Johnny." A trusting kid is turned off in a hurry and likely agrees and walks off. The educator can start off with an honest bargain by saying, "I want to help you and I appreciate your trust in wanting to talk to me about this. I promise to listen to you and I'll do that with an open mind and no opinion about how bad or good drugs may be for you. I also promise to try to understand your point of view, no matter what you tell me. In return, I want you to tell me the whole story of you and drugs. I'm not interested in your supplier, just your habit. After you've finished, we'll talk about where we go from there. That means that you may be able to settle this between us or that we both may have to get help from someone else."

The counseling contract cannot contain definite bargains with absolute confining limits on the teacher like, "If I tell you, do you promise not to tell anyone?" The temptation to agree with such a bargain has been experienced by any adult confronted by a youngster in distress, but experience has likewise taught that refusal to compromise is both immediately and ultimately the more respected position.

VII. *Counselor Role*. First, when the student reveals opinions on the absolutes of right and wrong, the teacher counselor has to avoid the traditional role of police or parent. The police are often perceived by youth as figures of arbitrary parental censure and prejudice and are often seen as dumb, uninformed, hypocritical, and impotent. Secondly, the teacher has to be aware of the testing procedure as the student reveals information (often erroneous) about "this pusher, dealer, pharmacist, doctor, or clinic." Possibly, the most difficult adaptation of the teacher/counselor is avoiding the censuring parent role and at the same time avoiding the role of an adult advocating illegal or self-destructive behavior. Some students suggest personal forms of blackmail such as, "If you tell any of this," or "If you only knew what your own kids were using." The temptation to reveal one's normal parental concern is obvious, but this ploy may only be a testing procedure by the student sincerely seeking help while trying to discover the educator's degree of prejudice against drug abuse.

*Summary of Student's Right to Confidentiality*

1. Maryland Public School Law 7–410 protects students who seek help from teachers, counselors, and other educators for overcoming drug problems.
2. A student can talk to a member of the school faculty about a drug problem and nothing said during the conference can be used against the student by the school, police, or courts.
3. The teacher or counselor is not required to report a student who comes for help with a drug problem.
4. Parents do not have to be notified that such a conference took place. However, every effort should be made to encourage students to involve their parents.

5. Parents do not have to be notified in the case of people under 18 seeking help for a drug problem from a physician, psychologist, hospital, or authorized drug abuse program.
6. When a student seeks help for a drug problem from a teacher, counselor, administrator, or other educator, no legal or school disciplinary action may be taken on the basis of this confidential communication. The confidentiality law protects a student's *statements* and the educator's *observations* during the help-seeking relationship.
7. The school officials cannot ignore illegal drug use. If a teacher, counselor, or principal finds a student bringing drug equipment to school, using, or carrying drugs, the educator must observe the drug laws and enforce school policy.

# References


Preface, pp. 15–17

[i]Lloyd D. Johnston and others, *Monitoring the Future*, National Institute on Drug Abuse (Washington, D.C.: Superintendent of Documents, U.S. Government Printing Office, 1986).

[ii]Ibid.

[iii]*A Study of Children's Attitudes and Perceptions about Drugs and Alcohol* (Middletown, Conn.: Weekly Reader Publications, 1983).

[iv]Ibid.

[v]*The Weekly Reader National Survey* (Middletown, Conn.: Field Publications, 1986).

[vi]Ellen Moorehouse, *Children of Alcoholics* (South Laguna, Calif.: National Association of Children of Alcoholics, 1986).

Chapter 1. The Drug Abuse Problem, pp. 18–37

[1]Lloyd D. Johnston and others, *Monitoring the Future*, NIDA (Washington, D.C.: Superintendent of Documents, U.S. Government Printing Office, 1986).

[2]Lloyd D. Johnston and others, *Use of Licit and Illicit Drugs by America's High School Students*, 1975–1984, NIDA (Washington, D.C.: Superintendent of Documents, U.S. Government Printing Office, 1985).

[3]"Adolescent Suicide," Boys' Town Communication and Public Service Division, undated pamphlet.

[4]Patrick C. McHenry and others, "The Role of Drugs in Adolescent Suicide Attempts," *Suicide and Life-Threatening Behavior* 13, no. 3 (Fall 1983): 131–35.

[5]Robert L. DuPont, Jr., M.D., *Getting Tough on Gateway Drugs* (Washington, D.C.: American Psychiatric Press, 1984).

[6]Sidney Cohen, M.D., "Marijuana and Learning," *Drug Abuse and Alcoholism Newsletter* 11, no. 3 (April 1982).

[7]Robert G. Niven, "Children of Alcoholics, A Special Report," *ADAMHA News* 10 (1984).

[8]Robert E. Hosty and Francis J. Elliott, "Drug Abuse in Industry," *Security Management* (October 1985): 53–56.

[9]Ibid.

[10]"Eight Fentanyl Analogs Banned on Emergency Basis," *Substance Abuse Report* 16 (November 1985): 1–2.

[11]*Drug Abuse, Drugs in a Chemically Dependent Society* (Washington, D.C.: Blue Cross and Blue Shield Associations, 1978), pp. 30–31.

[12]Linda Wheeler and Margaret Engel, "PCP: Cheap High, Heavy Burden," *Washington Post*, January 19, 1986; pp. A–1, 14.

[13]"Birth Defect Found in Infants of Heavy Smokers," *Washington Post*, October 12, 1985.

[14]"Cocaine-Cancer Link Told," *Los Angeles Times*, March 2, 1986; p. 2.

[15]DuPont, *Getting Tough on Gateway Drugs*; and D. B. Kandel, *Longitudinal Research on Drug Use: Empirical Findings and Methodological Issues* (New York: John Wiley and Sons, 1978).

[16]Coryl LaRue Jones and Robert J. Battjes, "The Context and Caveats of Prevention Research on Drug Abuse," in Coryl Larue Jones and Robert J. Battjes, eds., *Etiology of Drug Abuse: Implications for Prevention,* NIDA (Washington, D.C.: Superintendent of Documents, U.S. Government Printing Office, 1985), pp. 10, 11.

[17]Diane Jane Tessler, *Drugs, Kids, and Schools: Practical Strategies for Educators and Other Concerned Adults* (Glenview, Ill.: Scott, Foresman and Co., 1980), pp. 39–40; and DuPont, *Getting Tough on Gateway Drugs*, pp. 34–39.

Chapter 2. Why Young People Take Drugs, pp. 38–50

[18]Jones and Battjes, "The Context and Caveats," in Jones and Battjes, *Etiology of Drug Abuse*, p. 3.

[19]Therese Van Houten and Gary Golembiewski, *Adolescent Life Stress as a Predictor of Alcohol Abuse and/or Runaway Behavior* (Washington, D.C.: National Youth Alternatives Project, 1978), pp. 101–102.

[20]J. David Hawkins and others, "Childhood Predictors and the Prevention of Adolescent Substance Abuse," in Jones and Battjes, *Etiology of Drug Abuse*, p. 85.

[21]Diana Baumrind, "Familial Antecedents of Adolescent Drug Use," in Jones and Battjes, *Etiology of Drug Abuse* p. 30.

[22]Hawkins and others, "Childhood Predictors," in Jones and Battjes, *Etiology of Drug Abuse*, p. 77.

[23]Ibid., pp. 86–87.

[24]Jones and Battjes, *Etiology of Drug Abuse*, p. 7.

[25]Baumrind, "Familial Antecedents," in Jones and Battjes, *Etiology of Drug Abuse*, p. 30; and Hawkins and others, "Childhood Predictors," in Jones and Battjes, *Etiology of Drug Abuse*, p. 82.

[26]Baumrind, "Familial Antecedents," in Jones and Battjes, *Etiology of Drug Abuse*, p. 25.

[27]Ibid., p. 34.

[28]Hawkins and others, "Childhood Predictors," in Jones and Battjes, *Etiology of Drug Abuse*, p. 82.

[29]Cited in Tessler, *Drugs, Kids, and Schools*, p. 55.

[30]Ibid., p. 58.

[31]Hawkins and others, "Childhood Predictors," in Jones and Battjes, *Etiology of Drug Abuse*, pp. 79, 80, 83, 84.

[32]Ibid., p. 82.

[33]Ibid., p. 83.

[34]Ibid., p. 84.

[35]Ibid.

[36]Ibid.

Chapter 3. Whose Problem Is It? pp. 51–60

[37]Johnston and others, *Use of Licit and Illicit Drugs*, p. 110.

[38]Janice Castro, "Battling the Enemy Within, Companies Fight to Drive Illegal Drugs Out of the Workplace," *Time*, March 17, 1986, p. 52.

Chapter 5. Attacking the Problem, pp. 68–95

[39]Jason D. Baron, *Kids and Drugs* (New York: Putnam Publishing Group, 1983), p. 54.

[40]Robert Coles, Joseph H. Brenner, and Dermot Meagher, *Drugs and Youth* (New York: Liveright Publishing Corp., 1970), p. 55.

[41]Baron, *Kids and Drugs,* p. 60.

[42]Ibid., pp. 44, 49.

[43]Coles, Brenner, and Meagher, *Drugs and Youth*, p. 39.

[44]Baron, *Kids and Drugs*, p. 66.

Chapter 6. Preventing Student Drug Abuse, pp. 96–127

[45]David Murray and Cheryl Perry, "The Prevention of Adolescent Drug Abuse: Implications of Etiological, Developmental, Behavioral, and Environmental Models," in Jones and Battjes, *Etiology of Drug Abuse*, p. 237; and Hawkins and others, "Childhood Predictors," in Jones and Battjes, *Etiology of Drug Abuse*, p. 76.

[46]Brenna H. Bry, "Empirical Foundations of Family-Based Approaches to Adolescent Substance Abuse, " in Thomas J. Glynn and others, eds., *Preventing Adolescent Drug Abuse: Intervention Strategies*, NIDA (Washington, D.C.: Superintendent of Documents, U.S. Government Printing Office, 1983), pp. 154–55.

[47]*On the Sidelines: An Adult Leader Guide for Youth Alcohol Programs*, NIAAA (Washington, D.C.: Superintendent of Documents, U.S. Government Printing Office, 1981), p. 1.

Chapter 7. Prevention Materials and Activities in the Classroom, pp. 128–59

[48]Murray and Perry, "Prevention of Adolescent Drug Abuse," in Jones and Battjes, *Etiology of Drug Abuse*, pp. 237–39.

[49]Brian R. Flay and Judith L. Sobel, "The Role of Mass Media in Preventing Adolescent Substance Abuse," in Glynn and others, *Preventing Adolescent Drug Abuse,* p. 6.

[50]Ibid., p. 17.

[51]Hawkins and others, "Childhood Predictors," in Jones and Battjes, *Etiology of Drug Abuse*, p. 96.

[52]Ibid., pp. 98–99.

[53]Ibid., pp. 97, 98.

[54]Carole Ames, "Building Positive Self-Concepts in Students," unpublished materials used as part of presentation at Elementary Administrators' Conference, Montgomery County Public Schools (Easton, Md., March 26–27, 1981).

[55]Ibid.

[56]Ibid.

Chapter 8. Parent, Student, and Community Prevention, pp. 160–69

[57]*Young Children and Drugs: What Parents Can Do* (Madison, Wis.: Wisconsin Clearinghouse, 1984).

Chapter 9. Treatment Programs for Drug and Alcohol Abuse, pp. 170–84

[58]*Drug Abuse and Drug Abuse Research*, NIDA (Washington, D.C.: Superintendent of Documents, U.S. Government Printing Office, 1984), p. 8.

[59]Ibid., p. 54.

[60]J. Michael Polich and others, *Strategies for Controlling Adolescent Drug Use* (Santa Monica, Calif.: Rand Corp., 1984), p. 98.

[61]Ibid., p. 100.

[62]Ibid., p. 113.

[63]Ibid., p. 115.

# Bibliography

## Professional Resources


Ackerman, Robert J. *Children of Alcoholics: A Guidebook for Educators, Therapists and Parents*. Kalamazoo, Mich.: Learning Publications, 1978.

Allen, William A. *How Drugs Can Affect Your Life: The Effects of Drugs on Safety and Well-Being*. Seattle, Wash.: Thomas, 1983.

Allinson, Russel R. *Drug Abuse: Why It Happens and How to Prevent It*. Lower Burrell, Pa.: Valley Publications, 1984.

Anderson, Joan Webster. *Teen Is a Four Letter Word (A Survival Kit for Parents)*. White Hall, Va.: Betterway Publications, 1983.

Andrews, Theodora, ed. *Substance Abuse Materials for School Libraries: An Annotated Bibliography*. Littleton, Colo.: Libraries Unlimited, 1985.

Baron, Jason D. *Kids and Drugs*. New York: Putnam Publishing Group, 1983.

Brenton, Myron. *How to Survive Your Child's Rebellious Teens*. New York: Bantam Press, 1981.

*Chemical Dependency and Recovery Are a Family Affair*. Minneapolis: Johnson Institute, 1979.

Chu, G. "Drinking Patterns and Attitudes of Roominghouse Chinese in San Francisco." *Quarterly Journal of Studies of Alcoholism*. Supplement no. 6 (1972): 58–68.

Cretcher, Dorothy. *Steering Clear: Helping Your Child Through the High-Risk Drug Years*. Oak Grove, Minn.: Winston Press, 1982.

Crowley, James F. *Alliance for Change: A Plan for Community Action on Adolescent Drug Abuse*. Minneapolis: Community Intervention, 1984.

Deutsch, Charles. *Broken Bottles, Broken Dreams: Understanding and Helping the Children of Alcoholics*. New York: Columbia Teachers College Press, 1982.

Dinkmeyer, Don, and Dreikurs, Rudolf. *Encouraging Children to Learn: The Encouragement Process*. Englewood Cliffs, N.J.: Prentice-Hall, 1963.

Drug Council. *Facts About "Drug Abuse."* New York: Macmillan, 1980.

Duncan, David. *Drugs and the Whole Person*. New York: Wiley, 1982.

DuPont, Robert L., Jr., M.D. *Getting Tough on Gateway Drugs: A Guide for the Family.* Washington, D.C.: American Psychiatric Press, 1984.

Elkind, David. *All Grown Up and No Place to Go: Teenagers in Crisis.* Reading, Mass.: Addison-Wesley, 1984.

*Enhancing Self-Esteem and Achievement: A Handbook for Professionals.* Seattle, Wash.: Special Child Publishers, 1982.

Gold, Mark S. *800–Cocaine.* New York: Bantam Books, 1984.

Jenkins, Richard L., and others. *No Single Cause: Juvenile Delinquency and the Search for Effective Treatment.* College Park, Md.: American Correctional Association, 1985.

Leherman, Jonathan. *A Practical Guide for Handling Drug Crises.* Seattle, Wash.: Thomas Publishers, 1980.

Lingeman, Richard R. *Drugs from A to Z: A Dictionary.* 2d rev. ed. New York: McGraw-Hill, 1974.

Longstreet, Wilma S. *Aspects of Ethnicity: Understanding Differences in Pluralistic Classrooms.* New York: Columbia Teachers College Press, 1978.

Mack, John E., and Ablon, Steven L., eds. *The Development and Sustaining of Self-Esteem in Childhood.* New York: International Universities Press, 1983.

Manatt, Marsha. *Parents, Peers, and Pot.* NIDA. Washington, D.C.: Superintendent of Documents, U.S. Government Printing Office, 1979.

______. *Parents, Peers, and Pot II.* NIDA. Washington, D.C.: Superintendent of Documents, U.S. Government Printing Office, 1983.

Raths, Louis E. *Meeting the Needs of Children, Creating Trust and Security.* Columbus, Ohio: Charles E. Merrill Publishing Co., 1972.

Rose, Marc, and others. *Family Life Skills, Training for Drug Abuse Prevention.* NIDA. Washington, D.C.: Superintendent of Documents, U.S. Government Printing Office, 1984.

Schwartz, Richard H. "Frequent Marijuana Use in Adolescence: What Are the Signs, Stages?" *NASSP Bulletin* 69 (1985): 103–8.

Silvernail, David L. *Developing Positive Student Self-Concept.* 2d ed. Washington, D.C.: National Education Association, 1985.

Simon, Sidney B. *Negative Criticism, and What You Can Do About It.* Allen, Tex.: Argus Communications, 1978.

Singer, K. "Drinking Patterns and Alcoholism in the Chinese." *British Journal of Addiction* 67 (1972): 13–14.

Tessler, Diane Jane. *Drugs, Kids, and Schools: Practical Strategies for Educators and Other Concerned Adults.* Glenview, Ill.: Scott, Foresman and Co., 1980.

Van Houten, Therese, and Golembiewski, Gary. *Adolescent Life Stress as a Predictor of Alcohol Abuse and/or Runaway Behavior.* Washington, D.C.: National Youth Alternatives Project, 1978.

Wang, R. P. "A Study of Alcoholism in Chinatown." *International Journal of Social Psychiatry* 14 (1968): 260–67.

Weisinger, Hendrie, and Lobsenz, Norman M. *Nobody's Perfect: How to Give Criticism and Get Results.* New York: Warner Books, 1981.

Woodward, Nancy H. *If Your Child Is Drinking.* New York: Putnam Publishing Group, 1981.

## Student Resources

*Print*

Ahern, Thomas. "Chemicals and Driving Curriculum." Barnstable High School, Hyannis, Mass., n.d. Copies available from Tom Ahern, Barnstable High School, 744 West Main Street, Hyannis, MA 02601.

This photocopied driver's education unit contains pre- and post-tests and useful data on how drinking impairs driving ability. It also reviews Massachusetts drunk driving laws. (10–12)

*Alateen—Hope for Children of Alcoholics.* New York: Al-Anon Family Group Headquarters, 1973.

This publication elaborates the objectives, organization, and history of Alateen, and presents case histories of people who are helped through affiliation with the organization. It discusses the disease concept of alcoholism, with emphasis on the "family tendency" to develop alcoholism and the "family disease" approach to the problem. It also explains the twelve traditions of Alateen, recounts personal stories, and describes the various aspects of group planning and functioning. (10–12)

*Are You a Drug Quiz Whiz?* Kensington, Md.: National Clearinghouse for Drug Abuse Information, 1984. (9–12)

Burns, Marilyn. *I Am Not a Short Adult! Getting Good at Being a Kid.* Boston: Little Brown Publishing Co., 1977. (2–4)

Claypool, J. *Alcohol and You.* New York: Franklin Watts, 1981.

This book discusses teenage problem drinking, its causes and effects, and how to get help to overcome it. It provides information for senior high school-age youth on alcohol's effects on the body, problem drinking, alcoholism, and alcohol misuse by teenagers; and lists sources of information and help and further readings that may be especially helpful for young people. (9–12)

Donlan, J. *I Never Saw the Sun Rise.* Minneapolis: CompCare Publications, 1977.

A 15-year-old girl shares her journal writings about her dependency on drugs and alcohol and her treatment and recovery. The entries represent a year and a half of a teenager's life and were printed with only minor changes to the original manuscript. (7–12)

Donnahoo, T. *Who Needs Espie Sanchez?* New York: E. P. Dutton, 1977.

This novel tells the story of a young runaway Chicano girl who becomes involved with the Law Enforcement Explorer Group (a Los Angeles Police Department youth organization) and gains firsthand knowledge about teenage alcoholism. (9–12)

Dorman, N. B. *Laughter in the Background.* New York: Elsevier/Nelson Books, 1980.

This novel focuses on the problems of a young girl who tries, with unrewarding results, to understand and cope with the alcoholic behavior and attendant difficulties of her mother. After attending meetings with children of other alcoholic parents, she learns that she cannot assume responsibility for her mother's problems. (7–12)

Etons, Ursula. *Angel Dusted.* New York: Macmillan, 1979. (9–12)

*Feeling Better Together.* South Bend, Ind.: Pathway Memorial Hospital, 1985.

A coloring book with a simple story about a mother who drinks too much, how her problem affects the family, and how the mother finally goes to the hospital for help. The book emphasizes the feelings of the two young children in the family. (K–6)

Forrai, Maria. *Look at Drug Abuse.* Minneapolis: Lerner Publishers, 1978. (3–6)

Fort, Joel. *Addicted Society: Pleasure Seeking and Punishment.* Grover Press, 1981. (9–12)

Greene, Laura. *I Am Somebody.* Chicago: Children's Press, 1980. (3–6)

Hoff, Curtis. *Alcoholism: Hidden Addiction.* New York: Crossroad/Sebury, 1975. (10–12)

Howard, M. *Teenage Drinking: Did I Have a Good Time?* New York: Continuum Publishing Corp., Division of Seabury Press, 1980.

A fictional account of three teenagers, the story follows them through initial encounters with alcohol to the point at which alcohol causes some significant changes in their lives. It deals with alcohol-related problems faced by youth and offers alternative solutions. (7–12)

*How Much Do You Have to Drink Before You're An Alcoholic?* Kensington, Md.: National Clearinghouse for Drug Abuse Information, 1983.

A simple illustrated description of an alcoholic. (7–12)

*It's OK to Say No!* New York: Creative Child Press, 1984.

An activity book (dot-to-dot drawing, mazes, puzzles, word find) to educate young children about body safety. The book is most effectively used by a child under the supervision of an adult so that questions can be answered and adult and child can talk openly about the dangers of child molestation and abduction. (2–6)

Jackson, Bruce, and Jackson, Michael. *Doing Drugs*. Los Angeles: Martins Press, 1983. (9–12)

*Just Say No!* Kensington, Md.: National Clearinghouse for Drug Abuse Information, 1984.

A short, illustrated, easy-to-read pamphlet on peer pressure and ways kids can just say no to drugs and alcohol. (2–6)

Kenny, K., and Krull, H. *Sometimes My Mom Drinks Too Much.* Milwaukee: Raintree Children's Books, MacDonald Raintree, 1980.

Through simple narrative and dialogue, this illustrated book demonstrates the impact of a parent's alcoholism on the entire family, particularly the child. An elementary-school-age girl constantly struggles to cope with the effects of her mother's alcoholism. By explaining that her mother's strange behavior is caused by illness and by enlisting her aid, the father helps the child channel her thoughts into a positive direction. (4–8)

LeShan, Eda. *What Makes Me Feel This Way? Growing Up with Human Emotions*. New York: Collier Books, 1972. (4–8)

*Little Al's Coloring Book.* Lansing, Mich.: Alcohol Research Information Service (ARIS), 1984.

Very basic facts about alcohol are presented in coloring book format using a cartoon character named Al. (2–6)

Longoni, John. *Bombed, Buzzed, Smashed or Sober.* Boston: Little Brown and Co., 1976. (9–12)

Mann, Peggy. *Twelve Is Too Old.* Garden City, N.Y.: Doubleday and Co., 1980.

Jody dreads her twelfth birthday because she doesn't want to give up being a little girl and move on to adolescence with all its problems. Her parents are divorced; her mother worries about raising the family; and her sixteen-year-old sister is involved with marijuana and sex. The book ends with Jody's realization that being twelve isn't so bad after all. (5–9)

Robe, L. B. *Haunted Inheritance*. Minneapolis: CompCare Publications, 1980.

This mystery thriller recounts the adventures of Holly Blake when she spends the summer at Lyon House, a great mansion on Long Island. The story weaves in information for young adults about alcohol abuse, alcoholism, fetal alcohol syndrome, and Alcoholics Anonymous. (7–9)

Ryan, Elizabeth. *Life Is a Lonely Place: Five Teenage Alcoholics.* New York: Scholastic Inc., 1981. (7–12)

Schwandt, Mary Kay. *Kootch Talks About Alcoholism.* Fargo, N.D.: Serenity Work, 1984.

Kootch the worm helps young children understand three basic principles about alcoholism and alcoholics: (1) alcoholism is a disease, (2) alcoholism is no one's fault, and (3) alcoholics can recover. The 40-page coloring book also includes simple activities. (2–6)

Seixas, J. S. *Living with a Parent Who Drinks Too Much.* New York: William Morrow, Greenwillow Books, 1979.

This book is aimed at helping young adolescents with an alcoholic parent understand what is happening to them and to their parents. It describes alcoholism and the behavior of the alcoholic, and pinpoints the inevitable struggles that arise within family relationships. It also describes how others have dealt with similar problems and feelings, and gives specific suggestions for addressing the issues that surround family drinking problems. (7–12)

Snyder, Anne. *Kids and Drinking.* Minneapolis: CompCare Publications, 1981.

These short stories are based on the real experiences of children who become alcoholics during elementary school. The book includes questions and answers about alcohol, a short parent/teacher's guide, and a listing of other youth-related materials available from CompCare. It is suitable for older elementary and middle school children. (4–8)

Stasser, Todd. *Angel Dust Blues.* New York: Coward, McCann and Geoghegan, 1979.

This novel tells the story of a high school student, Alex, who becomes increasingly alienated from his successful parents who spend the winter in Florida while their son remains in the family home near New York with a housekeeper. Alex becomes involved with drug dealing through friends. As the trouble gets deeper, the only bright spot in Alex's life is a new girl friend who helps him see that he must accept responsibilities. (9–12)

Trivers, J. *I Can Stop Any Time I Want.* Englewood Cliffs, N.J.: Prentice-Hall, 1974.

The central theme of this book is teenage drug addiction, including alcoholism. A high school senior turns to alcohol after being arrested on a possession and sales charge. In the final scene, caught up in his own self-destructive pattern, having lost his family and girl friend, he states, "I can stop any time I want." (9–12)

Welch, B., and Vecsey, G. *Five O'Clock Comes Early.* New York: William Morrow and Co., 1982.

This account of the successful effort by baseball pitcher Bob Welch to overcome alcoholism includes the story of how he developed serious drinking problems and his treatment and recovery. (9–12)

Wilt, Joy. *Handling Your Ups and Downs: A Children's Book About Emotions.* Waco, Tex.: Word, 1979. (2–6)

*Films*

Elementary

*Alcohol and Drugs—How They Affect Your Body.* Barr Films, Pasadena, Calif., 1981. 20 min. (K–8)

*Almost Everybody Does.* Wombat Productions, Ossining, N.Y., 1970. 14 min.

Probes drug abuse from aspirin to heroin, relating its cause to the desire to relieve unpleasant feelings. (4–6)

*Cross Country High.* Barr Films, Pasadena, Calif., 1976. 14 min.

A young boy is influenced by older boys who challenge him to try a bottle of wine. (4–6)

*Drugs—A Primary Film.* Barr Films, Pasadena, Calif., 1972. 9 min.

Presents situations familiar to children to illustrate the correct use of drugs by the doctor and in the home. Reveals the danger of drug misuse and emphasizes the positive attitudes needed for a rich and healthy life. (K–6)

*Drugs Are Like That.* Benchmark Films, Briarcliff Manor, N.Y., 1972. 17 min.

Six episodes showing children the nature of addiction and the risks to health involved in drug consumption. (3–6)

*Fat Albert—Dope Is for Dopes.* McGraw-Hill Films, New York, 1976. 14 min.

(Learning values with Fat Albert and the Cosby Kids.) An episode showing the involvement of a schoolboy with his drugpusher brother. Teaches children to do the right thing, even though it might mean losing a friend. Presented by Bill Cosby. (5–7)

*Fat Albert—Ounce of Prevention.* McGraw-Hill Films, New York, 1976. 16 min.

Lucius has a drinking problem. Fat Albert and Lucius's parents come to his aid. (5–9)

*Feminine Mistake.* Pyramid Films, Santa Monica, Calif., 1978. 24 min.

(Suitable for some upper grade classes; screen carefully first. See Middle School/Junior High/Senior High list.)

*The Glug.* Service League of Northern Virginia, Inc., Arlington, Va., 1980. 14 min.

A dramatic film targeted for students 10–13 and for adults who work and live with them. Contains a very strong message: experimenting with alcohol can be very dangerous. (5–8)

*Is It Time to Stop Pretending?* American Automobile Association (AAA), Falls Church, Va., 1985. 5 min.

Nancy stops in the health office of her school to talk about her "friend" who is having a family problem involving alcohol abuse. The counselor suggests ways to approach the problem and gives Nancy a pamphlet about Alateen. Nancy isn't sure her "friend" would want to talk to anyone about the problem. At home she is confronted with a family argument involving alcohol abuse. (5–7)

*Lots of Kids Like Us.* Gerald T. Rogers Productions, Inc., Skokie, Ill., 1983. 28 min.

This film tells the story of Ben and his sister, Laurie, as they try to cope with their father's alcoholism. It is direct and supportive in its messages that "You are not alone" and "It's not your fault." (K–5)

*MTV: It's Your Right to Say "No."* American Automobile Association (AAA), Falls Church, Va., 1985. 4 min.

This specially prepared MTV (Music TV) presentation tells children it's all right to say no to alcohol. It urges them to resist peer pressure and not to ride with drivers who have been drinking. (5–7)

*The Octopuff in Kumquat.* American Lung Association, New York, 1975. 9 min.

An animated film about a mythical land that is invaded by an eight-armed, fast-talking pitch man, whose attempt to induce the citizens into smoking cigarettes is foiled by a group of children. (K–6)

*Story About Feelings.* American Automobile Association (AAA), Falls Church, Va., 1985. 10 min.

Live and animated scenes present the story of a boy named John, who begins smoking "to feel cool." John also uses drugs and alcohol to feel good, especially when he has problems that make him feel bad. Children tell the story, which depicts the deterioration in John's behavior and his relationships. The film emphasizes the message that substance abuse is an illness and not a moral weakness, as John is taken to a hospital because he took more pills and drinks than his body could handle. After treatment, John returns to a happy life with the help of his family and his cat Z. (5–8)

*Why People Smoke.* Pyramid Films, Santa Monica, Calif., n.d. 10 min.

Clever animated presentation of the antismoking side of the cigarette issue. (K–12)

Middle School/Junior High

*Alcohol and Drugs—How They Affect Your Body.* Barr Films, Pasadena, Calif., 1981. 20 min.

Begins by asking "Are you a polluter?" and goes on to explain ways in which alcohol and other drugs can pollute the body. (K–8)

*Alcohol, Drugs or Alternatives.* Barr Films, Pasadena, Calif., n.d. 26 min.

An exploration of alternatives to dependence upon drugs and alcohol. (7–9)

*Barbara Murray.* National Audiovisual Center, Washington, D.C., n.d. 15 min.

A young substitute teacher at Jackson Junior High School finds her class involved in a discussion of whether alcohol is "good" or "bad." The film touches on varied cultural and religious customs regarding alcohol, peer pressure, and attitudes toward drinking. (5–12)

*Drugs and Your Amazing Mind.* Alfred Higgins Films, Los Angeles, Calif., n.d. 16 min.

Explains the types of drugs, including alcohol, and their effects on the body. (6–9)

*Drugs: The First Decision.* BFA, New York, 1971. 9 min.

Explores the effects of drugs on young lives through interviews and reviews of case studies of teenage drug users. (6–9)

*Get the Message?* Gerald T. Rogers Productions, Inc., Skokie, Ill., 1984. 18 min.

Teaches children to analyze conflicting messages about drugs and alcohol accurately. The film also stresses the fact that saying no to drugs is everyone's right. (K–8)

*Like Father, Like Son?* National Audiovisual Center, Washington, D.C., n.d. 15 min.

Studying about drinking at Jackson Junior High School, Jim realizes that his own father is a problem drinker. He tries to talk to his father about his drinking. The film deals with social and problem drinking, physical and psychological effects of drinking, attitudes toward alcoholism, and where to find help. (5–12)

*The Party's Over.* National Audiovisual Center, Washington, D.C., 1976. 16 min.

A class at Jackson Junior High School discusses questions such as what the legal age of drinking should be, and when did you take your first drink. A group of young people crash a nondrinking party and one shows off by drinking too much. (5–12)

*Stoned: An Anti-Drug Film.* Learning Corporation of America, New York, 1980. 50 min. (8–12)

*Trigger Films for Alcohol Education.* University of Michigan, Ann Arbor, Mich., 1975. 2 min.

Six films of about 2 minutes each, designed to facilitate discussions that help young people clarify values and make firm commitments with respect to drinking. Suggestions for use are included in film can. (8–12)

*Understanding Alcohol Use/Abuse.* Walt Disney, Burbank, Calif., n.d. 12 min.

Demonstrates through animation how alcohol can disrupt the drinker's mental and emotional responses, explains the clinical physical effects of alcohol on the body, and explores the reasons people choose to drink. (6–12)

Middle School/Junior High/Senior High

*Alcohol, Drugs, or Alternatives.* Barr Films, Pasadena, Calif., n.d. 26 min.

An exploration of alternatives to dependence upon drugs and alcohol. (7–9)

*All Bottled Up.* Aims, Glendale, Calif., 1975. 11 min.

Animation used to interpret feelings expressed by teenagers whose parents are alcoholics. (9–12)

*All My Tomorrows.* Centron Films, Lawrence, Kan., 1979. 17 min.

Physiological and social effects of alcohol and barbiturates through the experiences of a teenage girl. (9–12)

*Angel Death.* Media Five, Los Angeles, 1980. 33 min.

A documentary view from the streets of PCP or "angel dust." (9–12)

*Born Drunk: The Fetal Alcohol Syndrome.* ABC Media Concepts, New York, 1979. 10 min.

Explains what alcohol can do to a developing fetus. (9–12)

*Comebacker—the Bob Welch Story.* Churchill Films, Los Angeles, n.d. 22 min.

Bob Welch, former Dodger pitcher, and his struggle with alcohol. (9–12)

*Death in the Fast Lane.* MIT Teleprograms, Northbrook, Ill. (9–12)

*Drugs, Drinking, and Driving.* AIMS Instructional Services, Hollywood, Calif. (9–12)

*Easy Way Out.* ACI Media, Inc., New York, 1971. 8 min.

Demonstrates the effects of marijuana and other drugs on the mental and emotional growth of the adolescent. (7–12)

*Feminine Mistake.* Pyramid Films, Santa Monica, Calif., 1978. 24 min.

The effects of smoking on a woman's body. Very effective presentation for both boys and girls. (6–12)

*I Am Joe's Heart.* Narcotics Education, Inc., Washington, D.C., 1979. 25 min.

Explains the heart's function, and portrays the effects of such factors as smoking. (8–12)

*I Am Joe's Lung.* Narcotics Education, Inc., Washington, D.C., 1979. 25 min.

Presents the functions of the lungs and the hazards related to their misuse, including smoking. (8–12)

*Is It Worth Your Life?* American Lung Association, New York, 1970. 24 min.

A physician demonstrates the physiological effects of cigarette smoking, explaining how smoking is a major cause of bronchitis, heart disease, and lung cancer. (7–12)

*It Can't Happen to Me.* Southerby Productions, Inc., Anaheim, Calif., n.d. 25 min. (9–12)

*Kevin's Story.* New Day Films, Wayne, N.J., n.d. 19 min.

The story of Kevin Tunnel, age 18, convicted of manslaughter and drunk driving for the death of an 18-year-old girl. As an alternative form of punishment, he was sentenced to speak about his accident for one year to high school students, parents, and teachers. This personal and powerful film is about his speech. (9–12)

*On Our Own.* Gerald T. Rogers Productions, Inc., Skokie, Ill., 1985.

Aimed at high school seniors and young adults, this film helps those who will soon leave high school for college, work, or military service become aware of their vulnerability to chemical dependency. (12–college)

*Reading, Writing, and Reefer, Parts I & II.* Films, Inc., Wilmette, Ill., 1978. 52 min.

An examination of the dramatic increase in the use of marijuana by American teenagers and adolescents, and its drastic effects on their lives. (7–12)